Nataliia Lazebna and Dinesh Kumar (Eds.)

Studies in Modern English

Nataliia Lazebna and Dinesh Kumar (Eds.)

Studies in Modern English

Würzburg
University Press

Impressum

Julius-Maximilians-Universität Würzburg
Würzburg University Press
Universitätsbibliothek Würzburg
Am Hubland
D-97074 Würzburg
www.wup.uni-wuerzburg.de

© 2022 Würzburg University Press
Print on Demand

Coverdesign: Holger Schilling

ISBN 978-3-95826-198-3 (print)
ISBN 978-3-95826-199-0 (online)
DOI 10.25972/WUP-978-3-95826-199-0
URN urn:nbn:de:bvb:20-opus-282426

Foreword

Globalization blurs the boundaries of human activities. English-language mediation of communication is interpreted in the humanitarian paradigm of knowledge within the linguistic and psycho-sociocultural study of speech activity in statics and dynamics with the priority of the cognitive and communicative paradigm. The socio-digitalized creative space of modern Human existence needs scrutinized scientific attention to the rapid development of global communication and its mediation. Digital discourse as the formation of new semiotic phenomena has crowned the rapid scientific and technological progress.

The interaction of natural English and programming languages is a significant sociocultural problem for both linguists and professionals in the field of computer technology, as well as for a wide range of amateurs. Programming languages are artificial, "unnatural" sign systems that are used in modern digital context for their integrated implementation in modern English text and discourse spaces. Focusing on the interaction of natural English and programming languages, the study by N.V. Lazebna and A.M. Prykhodko concentrates on this epistemic gap. The research by I.O. Chetvertak represents cyber aggression as a communicative pattern in English-language digital discourse. Within the concept of information structure proposed by C.E. Shannon, modern studies of digital discourse are based on changes both in the structure of the source of information and in the structure of the addressee of information. These changes imply that Human no longer appears as a carrier of communication code. The Machine on parity rights is also participating. The ethics of the behavior of Human and Machine and the manifestations of its marginality are considered by the researcher. In broader social and cultural terms, the role of modern English language is critically evaluated by K. Lut and A. Starenkova.

Taking as an example the ethical behavior of Human in the modern socio-political speech space aphoristic potential of presidential rhetoric, the linguist E.O. Kushch analyzes the speeches of President G. Bush Jr. Yu. Shtaltovna fosters the idea of modern English language and its democratization on the examples of English-language youth and their use of slang. The binary oppositions of Human behavior in the real and virtual worlds and its analysis by means of the English language testify to the multifaceted nature of this collective monograph. The diversity and variability of the English language are presented in the scientific research by J. Lubbungu, K. Nkrumah, I. Moong, A. Muyuni, S. Zimba in the Zambian version of the English language studied by scientists. Bilingualism is one of the most pressing issues of modern linguistic studies considered by A. Ribeiro Weng and P. Marco de Tony in the context of acquiring knowledge of English as a foreign language.

Z. Ali explores strategies for "memorizing" new English vocabulary and focuses on the ability of an individual to guess the meaning of a word from the context. Indian English-language studies in D. Kumar's paper historically outline the development of linguistic studies of English as a second foreign language.

Researchers' scientific achievements are systemic and valid in terms of evidence-based narratives, which reflect the transformational horizon of information theory, communication theory, and the theory of linguodidactics in modern English verbal, creative and digital environments. This monograph is undoubtedly distinguished by its multifaceted nature and significance for the European humanities as a whole. An integrated approach to the study of modern English as an open synergetic system requires a description of the relationship between verbal and nonverbal notions in digital space, respectively, verbal, nonverbal, and paraverbal notions of static-dynamic bipolar and binary oppositions in the structure of verbocreational, sociocultural and digital spaces.

A. M. Prykhodko
Prof., Habil. Dr. in Philological Sciences,
Chair of Theory and Practice of Translation
Zaporizhzhia Polytechnic National University

Preface

The existence of modern individuals on the globalized background of melted societies and cultures is mediated by the English language. To glorify the lingua franca of modernity, the book *Studies in Modern English* focuses on diverse linguistic patchwork. Following a tiny thread of language-related research, in the process of decorating this global English-language medium, this book transcends from the basic level of lexical unit analysis to discursive studies and reaches the point of learning and teaching aspects of English as a foreign language.

At present, from its novel practices and digital approaches, English Language Teaching has become a worldwide phenomenon. Its significance and importance are echoed in the countries where English is used as a second language which involves decidedly transdisciplinary as well as transnational paradigms that assume to return a new sense of importance to research in the field of the English language. In the present book, an attempt has been made to assimilate different aspects of the English language from the different countries of the world.

Often, voices unheard sound loudly. The authors from the underdeveloped countries have tried to focus on different aspects of English language development ranging from novice linguistic research to challenges in teaching and learning English, modern paradigms, and other perspectives, which may be beneficial to both learners and teachers.

This book will serve as a guide to all academicians, teachers, research scholars, students, and all those, who are constantly engaged in the search for novelties. *Studies in Modern English* as a representation of a holistic view of new trends and developments in the English language outline the individual views of the authors, their unique ideas, and the collective representation of innovative trends in modern studies of the English language.

Nataliia Lazebna
Privat Dozent, Habil. Dr. in Philological Sciences
TEFL Methodology Department
Julius-Maximilians-Universität,
Wuerzburg, Germany

Dinesh Kumar
Assistant Professor of English
Dyal Singh College,
Karnal, India

Acknowledgements

Studies in Modern English is the result of creative inspiration and a passionate trigger, which ignited my studies in metaphoric computer terminology in 2010 and further unwrapped into digital discourse studies.

My thanks and pleasure to acknowledge my inspiration from my academic advisors and inspirers: Professor Rusudan Makhachashvilli, Head of Romance Languages and Typology Department, Borys Grinchenko Kyiv University, Ukraine, and Professor Anatoliy Prykhodko, Head of Theory and Practice of Translation Department, Zaporizhzhia Polytechnic National University, Ukraine, and Professor Maria Eisenmann, Head of TEFL Department, Julius-Maximilians University of Wuerzburg, Germany. Their ideas are everlasting and they moved me to go global. Their bright thoughts and precious time granted deserve special mention. This project has been highlighted by a sparkle of my children's laugh, my husband's guidance, and my parents' everlasting support.

On behalf of co-editor of this book, Dinesh Kumar, Assistant Professor of English, Dyal Singh College, Karnal (India), I would like to thank the world's authors, whose voices have often been unheard. Global interaction with EFL teachers has inspired him and widened his horizon for further scientific researches in the field of EFL.

Nataliia Lazebna

Table of Contents

N. Lazebna / D. Kumar (Ed.), Studies in Modern English, Würzburg, 2022, p. 1-9. DOI: 10.25972/WUP-978-3-95826-199-0-1

Cyber aggression in the stance of communicative approach

Ievgeniia Chetvertak[*]

Abstract

The article deals with the notion of internet aggression (cyber aggression). It considers the mentioned term from both psychological and communicative approaches. The paper also provides detailed analyses of the cyber aggression in political discourse. The provided examples are taken from the speeches of politicians during the time of Covid pandemic. The author also identifies several types of cyber aggression.

Keywords: aggression, cyber aggression, xenophobia.

The empirical material is represented by English-language texts and text fragments from the political speeches during COVID pandemic.

Methods

- interdisciplinary method is implemented to consider cyber aggression in different fields of science;
- linguo-cognitive analysis focuses on communication aggression triggers;
- functional-communicative method to analyze grammatical, textual, and graphic properties.

General Discussion

The phenomenon of aggression, aggressive behavior of both humans and animals, is characterized by extreme complexity, a large number of factors that determine aggression and its forms; therefore, psychology has always paid considerable attention to their study.

One of the features of modern society is the rapid development of information technology and the creation of the Internet based on them. However, the new virtual environment (cyberspace), significantly expanding the possibilities of interpersonal communication, has led to the emergence of special forms of aggression – cyber-aggression ("cyber-aggression" or "cyber-harassment") in the Internet.

---

[*] Associate Professor, Translation Theory and Practice Department, Zaporizhzhia National Polytechnic University, Zaporizhzhia, Ukraine.

Studies of the phenomenon of aggression have always been accompanied by numerous attempts to define it accurately, the introduction of new terms for types and forms (species, subclasses) of aggression, criticism of which continues to this day. At the same time, the diversity and ambiguity of the term "aggression" and its categorical apparatus began to be perceived from the standpoint of pluralism, which, however, causes great difficulties in researching this phenomenon, especially in such little-studied area as cyber-aggression in the Internet.

A large number of monographs, review publications, dissertations are devoted to the study of the phenomenon of aggression and the definitions of this term in psychology. The most complete analysis of the concept of "aggression" and its categorical apparatus is given in the works of D. Richardson, R. Beron, ND Levitov, K. Lorentz, E. Frome, W. Gollicher, D. Dennen, B. Kreikha, K. Butner, T.G. Rumyantseva, M. Ramirez, D. Zillman, S.N. Yenikolopov and others.

Consider the main approaches to the formation and structure of the terms "aggression" and "cyber-aggression", as well as elements of their conceptual apparatus.

The founders of cyber aggression are Canadian high school teacher Bill Belsey (2005) and Nancy Willard (2003), an American lawyer and executive director of the Center for Safe and Responsible Internet Use who first introduced the term "cyberbullying".

The conceptual approach proposed in the works of B. Belsey and N. Willard caused an increase in the number of psychological studies of aggression in the Internet (cyber-aggression). A number of foreign authors (for example, M. Taki, P. Sle., S.Hymel, D. Pepler, H. Sim., S. Swearer, J. Raskauskas, A. Stolz, M. Hertz, C. David-Ferdon, especially in the United States) pay great attention to the study of various types (forms) of cyber-aggression; Chait J., Whitty M.T., and Blair C. consider definitions of terms that reflect the categorical apparatus of cyber aggression.

Analysis of publications showed that the terms used to describe aggression in the Internet largely depend on the point of view of the researcher. Therefore, today there is a significant diversity in the structure of the terms of cyber aggression, their definitions and categorical apparatus; and many terms, such as cyberbullying, electronic bullying, online social cruelty, online or internet harassment, online or Internet bullying and others (such as cyber-aggression, cyber-bullying, cyber-harassment, electronic aggression, online-aggression, online-harassment, etc.) are correlated with each other. Such terminological diversity, on the one hand, reflects the novelty of the rapidly developing scientific field, and on the other - significantly complicates the understanding and research of aggression in the Internet, which is also noted in works (McQuade, 2009, P. 17-19).

Difficulties in understanding and interpreting such terms in traditional and electronic forms of aggression of youth were pointed out in the work of J. Raskauskas and A. Stolz, which implies that an analysis of the structure of terms is needed, as well as a more accurate definition of them for cyberspace (Internet social networks).

An analysis of work related to the study of cyber-aggression also shows that the terms, despite differences in structure and spelling, in some cases have very close or identical definitions (e.g., "cyber-aggression", "cyber-bullying", "online-aggression", etc.), while analogues of these terms, as well as their definitions, are practically absent in the national scientific psychological literature.

The 4th, expanded, edition of the great psychological dictionary of B.G. Meshcheryakov and V.P. Zinchenko, published in Russia in 2009, also does not contain any concepts or definitions of cyber aggression. The English-Russian Dictionary of Psychology by E.V. Nikoshkova (2006), which is the first and only attempt at a systematic translation of English literature, contains several terms of the traditional conceptual apparatus of aggression (aggression, antisocial aggression, displaced aggression, physical aggression, self-oriented aggression, verbal aggression, aggressive, aggressiveness, aggression), but the formation of English-language psychological terms, component analysis of their structure in the dictionary is not mentioned, and no terms are given that reflect aggression in the Internet (cyber-aggression).

There are works on the creation of computer terms related to the Internet, but they do not consider the structure and formation of psychological terms of the categorical apparatus of cyber aggression.

Thus, the analysis of the main works on the problem of terminology and definitions of "aggression" and "cyber-aggression" in the Internet (cyberspace) shows that the issue of "cyber-aggression" in foreign psychological research is given much attention, but terminological differences and confusion remain. It was found that in national psychological studies of the phenomenon of cyber aggression in the Internet the problem of terminology and definitions of "cyber aggression" and its categorical apparatus was practically not considered, there is no research on component analysis of the structure and formation of cyber aggression terms, etc. This allows us to say that conducting research in this area is relevant.

From the analysis of the structure and dynamics of the development of English terms of the conceptual apparatus of aggression in the Internet (cyber-aggression) it follows that with the creation of the network there are terms that indicate aggression in it: Internet aggression, aggression in cyberspace. The term cyberspace was coined by the writer W. Gibson to refer to electronic space.

Modern terms of the conceptual apparatus of aggression in the Internet are mostly complex and can be written together, hyphenated or separately, for example: cyber-aggression, cyberbullying, cyber-stalking, electronic aggression, electronic bullying, online harassment. etc.

The given typical examples of English terms of aggression in the Internet show that the way of word formation in the categorical apparatus of cyber aggression is affixation, i.e. new words are created by joining word-forming affixes (Latin affixes - attached) to the creative basis.

Prefixes (Latin prefixes - attached to the front) cyber-, e- (electronic), I- (Internet), which belong to the group of Internet-related prefixes, are mostly used as word-forming affixes in English terms of cyber-aggression and its conceptual apparatus. The terms of the conceptual apparatus of cyber-aggression obtained in this way always have two word-forming elements: the creative basis and the affix. The main word (creative basis) is usually a noun and is located at the end. The words digital, electronic, Internet, mobile, online, virtual are written separately in compound terms.

The general purpose of prefixes is to use them in names and terms denoting electronic, computer products, information technology (Internet, etc.), services, etc. The use of these prefixes in relation to the conceptual apparatus of cyber-aggression is discussed below.

Initially, the prefix cyber- was used to form words related to computers, computer culture, information technology and virtual reality, or to denote certain futuristic concepts. Later, it was used more specifically, in terms of the Internet, online mode, etc. More recently, the prefix cyber- (cyber) also appeared in terms of the conceptual apparatus of aggression in the Internet (cyberspace), to describe suicide (cyber bullicide), when suicide is directly or indirectly related to online aggression, the formation of web-site names (for example, www.cyberbullying.org) and others.

The prefix e- means the word "electronic" and is used to define the terms e-mail, e-commerce, etc. In terms of the conceptual apparatus of cyber-aggression, English terms can be used both without the abbreviation of the word "electronic", for example, "electronic aggression", and with the abbreviation – "e-Bullying".

The prefix I- is not a general prefix, it was originally used to denote affiliation to the Internet, as well as in the branding of individual products, such as iPod, iTunes, iPhone, iLife, etc. In terms of the conceptual apparatus of cyber-aggression, the word Internet is used, as a rule, without abbreviations, for example, Internet aggression (Hinduja, 2008, P. 34).

The term online means electronic, network, non-autonomous mode of operation, when the computer is connected, for example, to the Internet. In terms of the conceptual apparatus of aggression on the Internet, it is also used without abbreviation, for example, online bullying.

The term "virtual" means virtual reality, i.e. imitation of reality. It is also used in terms of the categorical apparatus of cyber-aggression, such as virtual aggression.

The terms digital, mobile, SMS, etc. can be used in the conceptual apparatus of cyber aggression, for example: digital bullying, mobile bullying, SMS bullying.

Today it is safe to say that the 21st century is an era of globalization and multiculturalism. Thus, compared to 2000, the number of migrants in the world increased from 150 to 272 million. The hypothesis that such a migration jump is the result of the benevolent attitude of the population of the recipient countries towards foreigners seems to be true here. However, numerous studies prove that it is wrong. Moreover, today it is safe to say that globalization is contributing to the growth of xenophobia, as it exacerbates the problem of national identity and forces local societies to experience a loss of landmarks for self-identification. In today's globalized world, every society is forced to confront the dangers of others, which is observed both at the institutional level and in the manifestations of "popular anger". Xenophobic sentiments are most sensitive to media discourses and messages from key communicators.

The global sociological project World Values Survey presented the results of measuring the level of tolerance for various social groups in almost 100 countries (Mesa, 2018). The study showed that every four years the world public opinion about coexistence with people of other races, religions or nationalities changes dramatically. Usually this pattern is due to certain events in human history. For example, the peak of religious intolerance came during the "caricature scandal" of 2005-2006, which exacerbated the confrontation between the Muslim world and Europe.

In 2020, we see a new wave of aggression, namely, increasing xenophobia due to the COVID-19 pandemic. It is known that the coronavirus infection, the center of which became the Chinese city of Wuhan, spread rapidly around the world, killing more than 300 thousand people and causing a large-scale economic crisis. Thus, due to the collective fear for their own well-being and the desire to somehow counter the current threat, the world community has resorted to verbal discrimination against Chinese people in the Internet.

Verbal cyber-aggression is a form of psychological violence that manifests itself in the anonymous, public, and systematic use of hate speech against certain groups or individuals in the Internet. Such aggression is very dangerous, because it can lead to further social rejection and self-aggression of victims, to move to the level of physical clashes between persecutors and victims. Thus, such cyber-aggression can significantly affect the relationship that has been established between representatives of different national groups. That is why this phenomenon is studied in various scientific paradigms and planes - socio-psychological, cultural, social and communication. The discursive nature of xenophobia, the dependence of its manifestations on communication practices in the latest and traditional media makes this phenomenon a common object of social communication studies.

United States

On March 17, the President of the United States of America Donald Trump (@realDonaldTrump) published the following message on his page:

> The United States will be powerfully supporting those industries, such as Airlines and others, that are particularly affected by the Chinese Virus. We will be stronger than ever before.

The sudden change of the official name "COVID-19" to "Chinese virus" came at a time when the number of new cases in the United States has grown from several hundred to almost two thousand a day. Thus, we can assume that such manipulation, which was expressed in the national labeling of the pathogenic reality, was carried out in order to direct the fire of criticism of Americans not at the actions of the authorities, but at residents and migrants from China.

Trump's strategy was quite successful – 50% of commentators supported the position of their president. This is evidenced by the following posts:

"I can also call it Chinavirus. Which I will #sorrynotsorry", *"I actually prefer calling it the Kung Flu"* or *"I never thought our death would also be MADE IN CHINA"*.

In addition to contemptuous expressions, in the discussion we can also find calls for a complete boycott of any Chinese products and culture in general:

"You need to call it like it is, President. XI is not a friend. He is a killer. There will be millions when this is over that will never visit or buy Chinese again" and *"#Chinese Virus #Boycott China #Disgusting Animal Torturers Chinese #Evil Chinese CHINESE HAVE TO PAY"*. This indicates the activation of behavioral stereotypes, which, in addition to the negative cognitive component, also contain a pronounced guiding element.

Despite artificially inciting racial hatred, another 50% of commentators were quite negative about the president's words, prompting him to write a new tweet: *"It is very important that we totally protect our Asian American community in the United States and all around the world. They are amazing people, and the spread of the Virus is NOT their fault in any way, shape, or form. They are working closely with us to get rid of it. WE WILL PREVAIL TOGETHER".* This time, the number of discriminatory comments decreased to 41%, but the questions for the new post have not disappeared. The fact is that the president clearly divided his citizens into two camps: Americans (we) and Americans of Asian descent (they). Trump supporters immediately seized the opportunity, emphasizing the stated difference: "Bravo, Mr. President. It is important that we acknowledge that even though it is a CHI-NESE VIRUS. We, Christians, have forgiveness in our hearts. And we are willing to forgive them" or "Some Chinese Americans are CCP's supporters, while some are not. Therefore, I think not every Chinese American truly loves America. Many of them don't have any appreciation to America. It's better to have an ideology test or background checking before letting them immigrate to America". The binary opposition We/They, which is fundamental to xenophobia, has worked.

As we can see, the position of those in power as key communicators significantly affects the social orientations of society. If the president, who represents the interests of the state in the international arena, publicly justifies intolerant behavior, then the citizens feel free in its open expression.

In March 2020, the coronavirus was discovered in two of Britain's most influential people – Prime Minister Boris Johnson (@Boris Johnson) and the heir to the royal throne, Prince Charles (@Clarence House). That news shocked the local population, but provoked completely different reactions.

Following the official statement on the health of the Prince of Wales, the Clarence House residence said on its Twitter page that he was very grateful to everyone for wishing him a speedy recovery. Indeed, most of the comments under this post were filled with words of support for a member of the royal family. Moreover, none of them contained accusations against Chinese immigrants.

When Boris Johnson announced that his COVID-19 test was positive, the feedback from the population was virtually devoid of sympathy. The British have called on their prime minister to take responsibility for spreading the virus and take appropriate action to eliminate it. One of the proposed methods of overcoming the coronavirus was the complete cessation of any relationship with China: *"Stop trading with China, sick of their dirty viruses"*, *"DO NOT TRUST #COMMUNIST #CHINA. CUT OFF HUAWEI. DEPORT ALL #CHI-NESE #COMMUNISTS BACK TO CHINA"* and *"Whoever like to be #CCP friends or do businesses with them ... will pay a big price"*. However, such discriminatory comments accounted for only 7% of the total.

Therefore, we can conclude that the British population seeks answers not from the population of the country where COVID-19 was found, but from its parliament, the de facto legislature and executive, which failed to keep the virus out of the country.

Canada

On March 30, Canadian Prime Minister Justin Trudeau (@JustinTrudeau) posted a video message from Teresa Tem (@CPHO_Canada), the country's chief sanitary doctor. In her speech, she stressed the importance of social distancing in this difficult time for Canada. Despite the relevance of this message, citizens responded negatively. The comment section contained the following: *"Why is there no Canadians speaking for Canadians??? Who is this person?", "Investigate her whether she is a puppet of Chinese government", "Is she a Chicom spook?", "You're [Trudeau] a douchebag and your libtard government are a bunch of immigrants". "What is the reason for such aggression?"*

The fact is that Teresa Tem has argued for some time that there will be few cases of coronavirus in Canada, so there is no reason to panic and take drastic action. Many have speculated that Tem's inaction is due to a conflict of interest, as she herself is from Asia Minor, British Hong Kong. Then, on January 30, she tweeted, expressing concern about rising xenophobia on social media: *"I am concerned about the growing number of reports of racism and stigmatizing comments on social media directed at people of Chinese and Asian descent related to #2019nCOV # coronavirus... Racism, discrimination and stigmatizing language are unacceptable and very hurtful. These actions create a divide of #Us Vs Them. Canada is a country built on the deep-rooted values of respect, diversity and inclusion".* Most Canadians were outraged by the behavior of the chief physician, who said they were advocating political correctness instead of addressing pressing health issues.

In addition, commentators described the post as quite offensive, as it indirectly accused Canadians of racism that is not inherent in them. Meanwhile, according to the study, 14% of comments to this post were still discriminatory: *"Canada was not built on diversity. Diversity will destroy it though," "Stop lecturing Canadians about their own country. These are not deep-rooted values... Something you would know if you actually grew up in this country", "It's silly to go on pretending that under the skin we are brothers"* and *"If China wants us to stop spreading stigma maybe China should stop spreading diseases. We want Japanese and Koreans. We're not racists – Chinese are just terrible humans".* As we can see, the above statements contained offensive labels to denote members of a non-ethnic group. Thus, we can say that today, in the era of globalization, issues of race and nationality still play an important role.

During the coronavirus pandemic, verbal cyber aggression, unfortunately, has become a common reality today. According to the study, it manifests itself in various forms (from negative stereotyping, which actualizes the archaic opposition We/They, to discriminatory assessments and xenophobic appeals), setting different national groups against each other. And although the level of intolerance of the English-speaking population does not exceed 50%, the fears of Chinese people are absolutely justified, because in the last three months there have been more than a dozen cases of xenophobic aggression and real clashes between nations.

Now humanity is experiencing only the first wave of the pandemic. We can assume that the data we received are evidence of the beginning of mass discrimination. The higher the level of infection and the more active the economic crisis, the stronger the hatred for the people of the coronavirus country. That is why further monitoring of the online toxicity of the pandemic discourse is very important – both to understand the causes and information of aggression, and to combat it.

References

1.   Butyrina M. Xenophobia discourse: courses, scale and lessons for media. Ukraine. 2018. 260 p.

2.   Kuznezova O. Typology of xenophobia in Ukrainian mass-media. Visnyk Lvivskogo University. 2012. Vol. 33. P. 134–145.

3.   Melnichuk I. Some aspects of tolerancy in modern Ukrainian media. Visnuk of Zhitomir State University. 2008. Vol. 40. P. 19–25.

4.   Pogorezkii V. Xenofobia in Ukraine – myth or reality? URL: http://zolotapektoral.te.ua/ksenofobiya-v-ukrajini-mif-chy-realnist

5.   World Migration Report 2020. IOM, Geneva. URL: https://publications.iom.int/system/files/pdf/wmr_2020.pdf

6.   World Values Survey. URL: http://www.worldvaluessurvey.org/wvs.jsp

7.   Gagliardone I., Gal D., Alves T., Martinez G. Countering Online Hate Speech. UNESCO series on Internet freedom. Paris : UNESCO Publishing, 2015.

8.   Meza R., Vincze H. O., Mogos A. Targets of Online Hate Speech in Context. A Comparative Digital Social Science Analysis of Comments on Public Facebook Pages from Romania and Hungary. East European Journal of Society and Politics. 2018. Vol. 4. Issue 4. P. 26–50. DOI: 10.17356/ieejsp.v4i4.503.

9.   Rising levels of hate speech & online toxicity during this time of crisis. URL: https://l1ght.com/Toxicity_during_coronavirus_Report-L1ght.pdf.

10. Myers J., McCaw D., Hemphill L. Responding to Cyber Bullying: An Action Tool for School Leaders. Corwin Press, 2011. P. 216.

11. Limber S., Kowalski R., Agatston P. Cyber bullying: a prevention curriculum for grades 6 - 12. Hazelden Publishing, 2008. P. 146.

12. Shariff S. Cyber-bullying: issues and solutions for the school, the classroom and the home. Routledge Taylor & Francis, London and New York, 2008. P. 310.

13. Hinduja S., Patchin J. Bullying Beyond the Schoolyard: Preventing and Responding to Cyber bullying. Corwin Pr., London and New York, 2008. P. 254.

14. McQuade S., Colt J., Meyer N. Cyber bullying: protection kids and adult from online bullies. Greenwood Publishing Group, 2009. P. 221.

15. Raskauskas J, Stolz AD. Involvement in traditional and electronic bullying among adolescents. Dev Psychol. 2007; Vol. 43. P. 564-575.

Author's bio

Ievgeniia Chetvertak, PhD in Philology, Associate Professor at the Department of Translation, Zaporizhzhia Polytechnic National University, Ukraine. I. Chetvertak was born in Zaporizhzhya, Ukraine on 29 June, 1985. In 2007 graduated from Zaporizhzhia Classical University, Zaporizhzhia, Ukraine and got a Diploma of Teacher of English Language and Literature.

She was a teacher of English at Zaporizhzhya Technical State University, Ukraine; a post-graduate student at Zaporizhzhia National University, Ukraine; Associate Professor at National University "Zaporiz'ka Politechnika", 64, Zhukovskogo Street, National University "Zaporiz'ka Politechnika", Zaporizhzya, Ukraine. The areas of scientific interest: political linguistics, discourse analysis, terminology, translation studies.

I. Chetvertak has been the author of 51 articles published in local and international journals and a textbook Grammar Basis (2019).

N. Lazebna / D. Kumar (Ed.), Studies in Modern English, Würzburg, 2022, p. 11-17. DOI: 10.25972/WUP-978-3-95826-199-0-11

A Brief Historical and Present Perspective of ELT in India

Dinesh Kumar[*]

Abstract

English language is being taught as a second foreign language in India. For most of the learners in India, English still a foreign language or target language. The study of this language is important to fulfill different kinds of academic and professional requirements. Still, there is a big gulf between demand and supply for which the failure of the system is largely responsible as its main emphasis on to adherence to the foreign curriculum. The government tries to impose this curriculum on English teachers, but, in fact, the curriculum is outdated.

Keywords: learner, language, curriculum, foreign, majority.

It is a well-known fact that behind learning English, there are some set objectives as it is learnt either as a foreign language or as a second language. It is very much clear that any language, except mother tongue, is learnt with specific purposes and aims. No doubt, the Indians learn English as a second language or target language from the professional or career point of view. It is preferred as a medium, rather than a subject by a vast majority of parents in India. It is considered as somewhat a long term investment. It is because it determines their future prospective in India or abroad. It is also very unfortunate that there is a vast majority of illiterates in India who think English as a language of foreign countries.

English language in India is the result of a historico-political context. English started in India as not just as a foreign language, but as a much-hated language due to its association with the British colonizers. English today has come a long way from the despised instrument of oppression to the reluctantly adopted lingua-franca and the status symbol of the upper classes and its position today as a second language. But, for some in Indian society, it would not be an aberration to label it as first language. This is the main reason why the whole ELT paradigm also travelled the complete gamut at of modification is that the status of the language underwent constant re-invention.

There is no doubt in denying the fact that the Indian classroom was transformed because of the change in the environment of the learner in the last decades of the twentieth century when English started assuming the true status of global Language.

English as a subject is taught from two angles: general English and English for specific purposes. In the Indian scenario, the general English is offered at the secondary level, while the English for Specific Purposes is at the territory level either as an optional course in the

---

[*]   Assistant Professor of English, Dyal Singh College, Karnal, India, dineshkarnal1@gmail.com.

arts stream and mandatory in the technical institutions. English for specific purpose (ESP) has a number of sub-division that depends upon the purpose, academic or professional.

The term, professional English, has been used as an umbrella term, which is used for practical purposes. It includes varied purposes- oriented courses that comprise English for international business, for import and export, for banking and international trade, for science and technology, for internet and computers, nursing, pharmacy, the International media and many more.

As far as English Language Teaching in the Indian context is concerned, no doubt, it started accidentally, but at present, it has become so vital and significant that it is impossible to continue without it. Once it was recognized as the official language, but now it is considered as the language of opportunity. People are ready to spend a considerable amount of money as well as energy on coaching and material because of its practical usefulness that is definite and certain.

The beginning of liberalism in Indian economy is the first great factor for learning of English language in India. From the professional job point of view, the whole spectrum in the field of job opportunity has been changed. It can be perceived through those students who have specialized in English even after joining civil services. The call centers in India need some trainers to equip their employees with better communication skills. Besides, there are some multinational companies that are busy in recruiting marketing staff who requires to speak English. In addition to it, the medical transcriptions centers are also in the need of translators and reporters. Those, who want to go abroad, are in the need of professional help for IELTS.

This change was first perceived at various levels such as-social, political and economic. Very soon, the idea that English is the passport to success in India and in abroad. That is why, it is observed that nowadays many people want to opt for English. In the beginning, only a few groups were using English in their everyday life. On the other hand, the middle-class people thought that it should be used only for official purposes. They also wished to use it to leave an impression upon the other classes. The lower classes found it beyond them. But, the government has been trying hard to educate the lower classes through the government school of India, but the lower classes did not have any exposure to this language.

During the 1990s, a change was witnessed in the whole paradigm which was possible only through liberalism in the economy. It resulted in the establishment of some multinationals that were responsible for the varied development such as different jobs and opportunities that focused on fluency of English. The process was facilitated by a number of channels on the television, increase in the English publications and, moreover, for the Indians the international lifestyle was tempting.

There is no doubt in denying the fact that advancement and growth in the field of ELT methodology in foreign countries took a long time to come to India. Like other EFL countries, the growth and development of ELT in India is closely connected with factors other than pedagogic. In the Indian scenario, English cannot be labeled as a foreign language as it was in the past when teaching was to take apprehension of all factors including pedagogic or others. Two components are vital and significant in observing the elaboration of ELT which are different in case of ELT in India and ELT in other countries.

As far as the question of developing the ELT pedagogy is concerned, it developed primarily in the Western countries where the social and political environment was entirely different as the status of English was fixed. But, in the case of the Indian context, the ELT pedagogy relies on the subtle and not so-subtle which the status of English keeps changing all the time. In the case of position of English in Indian society, no diagrammatic manifestation can be complete without taking into account its fluid nature.

In India, ELT took a long time to spread its roots and the reasons for this are numerous. The first and the foremost among these is that English caught the attention of the policy makers, administrations and teachers around the year 1980. So, the significance of ELT in India was realized after the three decades of India's independence. English as a subject was kept only for one year in it. It was for this period that English was part of teacher training for school teachers. The teachers did not get any training when they were newly recruited. In the orientation and the refreshers courses meant for the teachers, ELT does not have any space.

In recent years, only the programmes like CELTA and other have been introduced by British council. But, the fact is that these programmes are costly and that teachers do not want to spend money on them. The other main reason is that the examination system makes an emphasis on achievements rather than performance. This system does not strongly advocate its focus on the issue of fluency or proficiency, but the main concern is grading and positions. Consequently, the role of a teacher in the classroom has been reduced to merely of a facilitator of examination instead of linguistic or communicative proficiency.

It goes without saying that English Language Teaching in India, despite its slower rate of advancement, has been widened in its approach and methods. As a result of this, more and more are intend to reach the end of ELT. Despite the slow growth of ELT in India, it is now in step with the rest of the world today. ELT can be seen emerging in three transient stages as for as the question of methodology is concerned according to the different levels of Paradigms.

The first level refers to those situations which are run by the government, especially primary, secondary and high schools. The main aim of these is to impart education at reasonable and subsidised levels to the public, so ELT and learning cannot be kept at the widest end. The main reason behind it is that teachers do not have the latest facilities of research as well as the materials for economic and geography reasons. In the rural and remote areas, these institutions are the only sources to fulfill the basic requirements of people. There is a difference in the urban area as their institutions are many towards up gradation through teacher training, improved resources and syllabus modification. In a couple of decades, the level of ELT is going to be more communicative in nature integrated fully with language and literature.

The semi-government institutions can be included at the second level as are assisted through government funding by private managing bodies. The undergraduate and post-graduate colleges, and universities can also be assimilated into the semi-institutions. These teachers are conscious of what the learners want. They can use other methodology by a harmonious blending of interaction and communication in the classrooms. The lectures based on the talk-chalk are mostly teacher- oriented. The main advantage of this is that the present teachers are seeking alternate methodology as they are trying to change their teaching practices because of the mixed bag of teaching practice, the institutions can be seen ranging from indifferent to private.

At the third level, we can include the pure private sector where the students are charged a fixed amount of money to make them proficient in English learning for a particular period of time. As they have only particular tenure of time in which they complete the syllabus, they use the latest equipments including multimedia, software and interactivities. Since in these academic fields, the jobs are few, which compel an increasing number of qualified teachers to rush these places. As regarding the question of methodology, the teachers' profile gets younger and younger that result into the increasing amount of experimentation and innovations.

On the one hand, the teachers belonging to the first level are satisfied, whereas the teachers of the second level are considerably influenced by the third level in order to get clear IELTS, as they are in the need of employment. For this, they generally join academies in addition to their undergraduate classes.

The young teachers, after joining academies, try to make the full use of the latest teaching aids and materials in order to gain fluency as soon as possible. Their teaching methodology undergoes a change at their place of work. It is because they tend to use the interactive, task-based and communicative methods in comparison to the usual lecture methods. In India, parents of learners form a significant and vital part of the teaching paradigm. In the beginning, any kind of change in the teaching methodology would cause some opposition from them, but the age-old practices are recommended by the administrative body. The parents, in the midst of the changing winds, accept the global status of English. As a result of that, at present, parents encourage innovation and experimentation in the classroom.

After comparing the situation of ELT in past, the learners can be found in search of such stimulation while attending their regular classes. It is to be observed after when they attend interactive classes at the academy. These are some radical and drastic changes that one can perceive in the absence of the right context. The Communicative Language Teaching was an utter failure with its advent in India for the first time in 1980s. But, at present, this context has gained momentum that has made all the learners receptive who are the source of inspiration for more and more learned-centred classes.

Since 2000, socio-economic factors have played a significant and vital role. The result of this is that we find a big and drastic change full of dynamism. The mindset of the English learners has changed due to the liberalisation in the Indian economy. There is a dire necessity for English learning at call centers, shopping malls and trade fairs as their priority is of young and vibrant learners who are fluent in English language. The continuous emergence of the institutes and academics in the third category offer the whole-range of proficiency in English language from clearing IELT speaking fluently. Moreover, by giving a wide-range of exposure to English, internet has played a significant and vital role. These factors, have paved the way for the deadlock that CLT found in recent years.

Communicative Language Teaching has its origin in changes that occurred in the field of linguistic and psychology of learning in United States during the mid 1960s. At the same time, when the linguistic theory underlying audiolingualism was being defied in America, the theoretical assumptions underlying situational language teaching in Britain were also being questioned. Naom Chomsky's Syntactic Structure (1959) demonstrated the inadequacies of structuralists linguistics.

It also highlighted the uniqueness and creativity of individual utterances. Around the same time, British Applied Linguists emphasised the functional and communicative potential of language. The result of this revolutionary idea was a shift from focus on language teaching from mastery of structure to developing communicative proficiency. The strong advocates of this view such as Christopher Candin and Henry Widdowson drew on the works of British functional linguistics like Halliday and the philosophical works of John Searle as well as John Austin provided the further impetus.

The process of changed thinking in language teaching provided the basis to theorists like D.A. Wilkins to work out a functional or communicative definition of language and devise communicative syllabus for language teaching. All the developments were, later on, consolidated as Communicative Language Teaching. CLT starts from the theory of language as communication. As far as the goals of CLT are concerned, Richards says that the goal of language teaching is to develop what Hymes referred to as Communicative Competence. The major function of language is communication. It is not enough to acquire the skill of putting words together to construct grammatically acceptable sentences. What is much more important is the acquisition of the linguistic competence to achieve results such as successfully 'arguing', 'persuading', 'inviting', 'agreeing' even disagreeing without being 'disagreeable', 'accepting', 'declining' an offer or gift without being impolite or arrogant describing, defining or reporting.

Widdowson has given a detailed exposition to the ideas underlying the concept of Communicative Language Teaching by manifesting the relationship between linguistic system and communicative value in text and discourse. More recently, Canole and Swain in their analysis of Communicative Competence have identified four dimensions of Communicative Competence. They consider these dimensions essential both for theoretical understanding of communication and its practical application to language teaching.

These four components are as follow:

(a) Grammatical Competence: It includes Chomsky's concept of linguistics.
(b) Sociological Competence: This refers to an understanding of social context in which communication takes place including roll relationship, the shared information of the participants and the communicative purpose for their interaction.
(c) Discourse Competence: It refers to the interpretation of individual message event in terms of their interconnectedness and how meaning is represented in relationship with the entire discourse.
(d) Strategic Competence: It generally refers to the copying strategy that communicators employ to initiate, terminate, maintain, repair and redirect communication.

Characteristics of CLT

In his book, *On Teaching Methodologies*, Stern observed that one of the recurrent features of Communicative Language Teaching is that it pays systematic attention to functional as well as a structural aspect of language. In this method of teaching, learners are engaged in problem solving tasks in groups and pairs. The learners have to communicate within their groups/within the linguistic resources available to them. It is very well realized that there may be very different kinds of communicative functions. But, what is common to them is that at least two parties are involved in an interaction or transaction of some kind of where one party has an intention or transaction of some kind and other party expands or reacts to that intention. The target linguistic system is made to learn through the process of struggling to communicate.

In the Communicative Language Teaching method, teachers help learner in any way that motivates them to work with the language. Communicative competence is the desired goal and language is created by the individual often through trial and error. Translation may be used where students are in the need or benefit from it. Sequencing is determined by any consideration of content, function, or meaning which maintain interest. Fluency and acceptable language is the primary goal in CLT; accuracy is judged not in terms of the abstract but in context. The role of a learner as negotiation between the self, the learning process and the object of learning emerges from and interact with the role of joint negotiation within the group and within the classroom procedures and activities that the group undertakes.

In CLT, a teacher facilitates the communication process among the participants in each group and between these participants and various activities and texts. It also acts as an independent within the learning teaching process.

There are certain principles that underlying CLT practice and learning theory are illustrated as below:

(a) Communication Principle: activities that promote real communication promote learning.
(b) Task Principle: activities in which language is used for carrying meaningful tasks promote learning.
(c) Meaningful Principle: Language that is meaningful to the learner supports the learning process.

In this way, after making a close and incisive study of both the aspects, ELT and CLT, we can safely and rightly aver the fact that CLT as an approach is marked by the flexibility of procedures which allows individual interpretation, variation and adaptation to different situations. This is what makes it a more reasonable approach as compared to most other methods. This approach is more humanistic rather than mechanical by promoting interactive processes of communication. CLT also appeals as a more productive approach.

References

1.   Indira, M. (2003) The *Suitability of Course Book in Engineering Colleges for Developing Communication Skills*: A Study. Hyderabad: Central Institute of English and Foreign Languages.

2.   Spolsky, R. *Educational Linguistics: An Introduction*. Mass: Newbury House, 1978.

3.   Srivastava, A.K. (1990) Multilingualism and school education in India: special features, problems and prospects, in Pattanayak. International Journal of Scientific and Research Publications, Volume 4, Issue 5, May 2014 ISSN 2250-3153 www.ijsrp.org

4.   Macaulay, L. (1935) *Speeches by Lord Macaulay with his Minute on Indian Education.* Oxford: Oxford University Press.

5.   Kachru, B. (1986) *The Indianisation of English: The English Language in India.* New Delhi: Oxford University Press.

6.   Pennycook, A. (1994) *The Cultural Politics of English as an International Language.* Harlow: Longman Group Ltd.

7.   Howatt. B. (1984) *A History of English Language Teaching.* Oxford: Oxford University Press.

8.   Gupta (1996) "Reading A: English and empire: teaching English in Nineteenth century India" in *Learning English: Development and Diversity*, London: Routledge.

Author's bio

Dinesh Kumar has presently been working as an Assistant Professor of English at Dyal Singh College, Karnal (INDIA) for the last 15 years. Besides, 40 research papers to his credit in reputed National as well as International Journals, his thrust areas of research comprise of Feminism, Dalit Literature, Comparative Literature, Commonwealth Literature, post-colonialism, Linguistic, Eco-feminism, Translation Study and Post-modernism. In addition to it, he has also contributed 20 book chapters on different topics. He has three books to his credit as a sole author-George Orwell's Social Vision: A Critical Study (ISBN 978-93-87646-79-7); and Voices in Literature (ISBN 978-93-87276-79-6), Feministic Ethos in Pre-Independence and Post-Independence Indian Literature: A Comprehensive Study from Lambert Publication, Germany (ISBN 978-620-3-921908). He has also reviewed two books of foreign professors-first, English Language as Mediator of Human-Machine Communication by Natalia Lazebna, Associate Professor, Zaporizhizhia Polytechnic University, Ukraine with ISBN 978-81-948672-1-0. and the second is a poetry book, Drops of Intensity by an Italian poet, Gerlinde Staffler. Being an active member in the editorial boards of different National and International journals since 2014, he is rendering his services as an editor and a reviewer in national and International Journals

N. Lazebna / D. Kumar (Ed.), Studies in Modern English, Würzburg, 2022, p. 19-39. DOI: 10.25972/WUP-978-3-95826-199-0-19

Differences and Similarities between the Fields of Bilingualism and Second Language Acquisition

Ana Kellen Ribeiro Weng,[*] Plinio Marco De Toni[†]

Bilingualism

According to Liddicoat (1991, p. 1), bilingualism is "the ability to use two (or even more) languages". Yet, to this author, in order to assess a bilingual's language competence, the four skills listening, speaking, reading, and writing need to be taken into account regarding each language spoken by the individual. Moreover, Grosjean (2008, p. 10), concerning bilingualism, states that it "is the regular use of two or more languages (or dialects), and bilinguals are those people who use two or more languages (or dialects) in their everyday lives". Besides that, with respect to the evaluation of bilinguals' competence in language, Grosjean defends that it should encompass the languages spoken by the bilingual as in the same way these languages are used by him or her on his/her daily basis. The author also presents two views of the bilingual person such as the monolingual, which consists of two distinct language systems as if this individual is, actually, the junction of two monolinguals and as consequence, this concept of bilingualism led to the notion of a "real" bilingual with well-balanced language skills regarding the languages this person speaks. Also, as it consists of two separate language competencies, if one accidentally gets in touch with the other it is the result of "borrowings" and "code switches". (op. cit., p. 12). Consequently, Grosjean states his opinion about how he disagrees with this view and in addition to that, the author brings up the "wholistic" view of bilingualism that consists of a single and unique language setting in which the languages spoken by the bilingual interact, forming one language system. Therefore, according to the author, the "bilingual is a fully competent speaker-hearer" and besides developing competences in both languages the speaker can also develop another one combining those two in order to meet his/her needs.

Yet, Myers-Scotton (2006) claims that what stimulates bilingualism is the contact among those who do not share the same first language (L1). Besides, the author draws attention to the fact that "bilingualism is a natural outcome of the socio-political forces that create groups and their language flourish" (p. 9). In addition, Baker (2011, p. 12), when regarding bilingualism affirmed that "language is not produced in a vacuum", to this extent, the people involved as well as the environment need to be taken into consideration. Additionally, the bilinguals' use of language varies according to their contexts and purposes (GROSJEAN, 1997). In this regard, there are different ways of referring to bilingual individuals and, as claimed by Butler and Hakuta (2004, p. 115), the classification of them into categories based

---

[*]   Masters Student in Letters, The Midwestern State University, Brazil.
[†]   Associate Professor, Department of Psychology, The Midwestern State University, Brazil.

on "linguistic, cognitive, developmental and social dimensions" consists of the field's preferred activity, that is, the authors emphasize that when classifying the bilinguals, the relationship between the proficiency of both the L1 and the L2, the age, and the status of a language in society need to be considered. Therefore, in order to present a few of them, Moradi (2014) puts together some of the bilinguals' classifications such as the early/late; simultaneous/successive; balanced/dominant; compound/coordinate/subordinate; folk/ elite as well as additive/subtractive. Hence, according to BaetensBeardsmore (1986, p. 28 *apud* MORADI, 2014, p. 108), the early bilingual acquires languages "in the preadolescent phase of life", whereas the late bilingual acquires one language before and the other after this period of preadolescence when the L1 experiences can reflect into the learning of the L2 (MORADI, 2014). As a consequence, the early bilinguals tend to have a "native-like linguistic competence" in regard to the languages they acquire in this stage. Also, early bilingualism can be divided into two categories: simultaneous and successive. The first corresponds to the acquisition of two languages concurrently under the age of eight and the latter occurs when the early bilingual has in part acquired the L1 and then begins to learn L2.

Peal and Lambert (1962 *apud* MORADI, 2014, p. 108) explain the difference between a balanced and a dominant (unbalanced) bilingual. The balanced bilingual is the one whose "proficiency and mastery" of the languages acquired are equal. While the unbalanced one tends to develop more in one of the languages acquired.

In respect to compound, coordinate and subordinate bilinguals, Weinreich (1953 *apud* MORADI, 2014) claims that they concern the bilinguals' linguistic codes and the meaning units. Thus, whereas a compound bilingual has only one meaning unit to more than one linguistic code (language acquired), the coordinate has different meaning units according to the linguistic codes the person possesses, that is, for each language, there is a specific meaning unit. Yet, the subordinate bilinguals have different linguistic codes, however, they only have one meaning unit that needs the L1 to be accessed.

Fishman (1997 *apud* MORADI, 2014, p. 109) points out that the social, as well as cultural aspects, are also involved when classifying types of bilinguals, thus, the author presents the folk and the elite terms. Therefore, the folk label is used in regard to those who speak a non-dominant language from a minority group when compared to the "predominant language" of a certain society, while elite bilinguals are the ones who speak languages that are considered relevant and beneficial inside a given community.

Finally, when it comes to additive and subtractive bilinguals, Lambert (1994 *apud* MORADI, 2014) states that the former relates to the person who learns an L2 and does not stop using the L1, therefore, both languages keep developing. On the other hand, the subtractive term concerns the bilingual whose L1 tends to be lost in the process of learning an L2.

In addition, another point that has been studied in this field is the linguistic mode, that according to Grosjean (2008), it is the condition in which the bilinguals activate or, consequently, deactivate a given language regarding the bilingual needs. Yet, what has also been researched is how a chosen linguistic mode can affect a bilingual's language behavior.

Second Language Acquisition

Prior to the establishment of the second language acquisition (SLA) as theory, the concerns regarding how other languages than the first one were acquired used to be linked to pedagogical issues as well as the theory that has originated from "a practical orientation to language teaching" (VANPATTEN; WILLIAMS, 2014, p. 17). In addition to that, the authors state that before the 1990s the SLA theory explanation relied on both behaviorism and structural linguistics, thus the research at that time was "essentially descriptive" (LARSEN FREEMAN, 1991, p. 315). Therefore, since its beginning, this theory has been receiving theoretical influence from many varied fields in order to discuss how people acquire nonprimary languages and, more specifically, why not everyone succeeds to do so (LARSEN FREEMAN, 2000).

In accordance with Gass (2013), SLA is a discipline which "refers to the process of learning another language after the native language has been learned" and when it comes to L2, it means "the acquisition of a second language both in a classroom situation, as well as in more 'natural' exposure situations" (2013, n.p.).

Moreover, to Rod Ellis (1994), "the term 'second' is generally used to refer to any language other than the first language". In respect to SLA perspectives, the author also distinguishes the *naturalistic* ("when the language is learnt through communication that takes place in naturally occurring situations") and the *instructed* ("through study, with the help of 'guidance' from reference books or classroom instructions"), highlighting that both are being considered based on the sociolinguistic view, that is, taking into account the environment and activities one is engaged with. The author also differentiates *second* and *foreign language acquisition*. The second corresponds to a language, other than the mother tongue, which is spoken in a given community, while the *foreign* "takes place in settings where the language plays no major role in the community and is primarily learnt only in the classroom" (p. 12). It is important to point out that acquisition and learning are terms used interchangeably by the author.

Additionally, in order to understand what SLA's aim is, it is necessary to master some of the Chomsky concepts such as *competence* and *performance*. The former refers to the innate capacity humans have to develop language and the latter is about how this language is used (ELLIS, 1994). Second language acquisition's goal, thus, is to describe and explain the "learners' linguistic or communicative competence" (p. 15). As stated by Ellis, that only can be done when the learner's performance is scrutinized. Hence, SLA focuses on the analysis of the language produced by the speaker in order to comprehend his/her competence. To do so, one of the first methods was the analysis of the learners' errors and by errors, the author means "a deviation from the norms of the target language" (p. 51).

To better understand how this field of research works, Ellis (1994, p. 18) presents "a framework for investigating L2 acquisition" consisting of four areas of the SLA theory that have specific aspects in each one to be approached by the researcher according to his/her aims. That being said, the areas are *the characteristics description of the language learners* in which four aspects can be analyzed considering the learner performance: the errors, acquisition orders and developmental sequences, variability, and pragmatic features. The second area is the *learner's external-external factors* which corresponds to the learner's social context, input, and interaction. The third: *the learner-internal mechanisms* involving the L1 transfer, learning processes, communication strategies, and linguistic universals. Finally, the fourth: *the language learner* that consists of general factors such as motivation, and the learner strategies.

Furthermore, another author that has also been contributing to the field of SLA is Krashen, whose Monitor Theory regarding second language acquisition has its foundation based on five hypotheses as to *the acquisition-learning distinction, the natural order hypothesis, the monitor hypothesis, the input hypothesis,* and *the affective filter hypothesis.* The first corresponds to acquiring ("pick up" a language", a "subconscious process") and learning (the "conscious knowledge about a language"), which are the two mechanisms adults have to develop competence in a given language (KRASHEN, 1982, p. 10). The second refers to the existence of an acquisition order of grammar structures. The third, on one hand, refers to the acquisition and learning of a second language, however, it specifies that acquisition happens in the first stage when the sentences are starting to be produced as well as it is related to fluency. On the other hand, learning plays a role in correcting the utterances that are about to be or are already made, as a monitor. Nevertheless, in order to use this monitor, it is necessary to consider three conditions such as *time, focus on form,* and also, it is of fundamental importance that the "performers" *know the rule* of a language; it is said, however, that even when all these conditions are met, the monitor may not work fully.

Krashen also claims that there are three types of performers considering the Monitor Hypothesis: the *over-users* who think there is the obligation of knowing all the rules and tend to show they are afraid to make mistakes; the *under-users* who do not care about making mistakes and do not correct themselves, only if they feel something is not right, and the *optimal* who knows how to balance the conscious knowledge and uses it in a way it does not interrupt the performance. The fourth hypothesis with the aim of answering one of the most relevant questions of the field: *"how do we acquire language",* is based on the idea that acquisition happens when an amount of input, extra than what is already acquired by the performer, is given and can be understood by taking into consideration the context "which includes extra-linguistic information, our knowledge of the world, and previously acquired linguistic competence" (KRASHEN, 1985, p. 80). The last consists of the affective filter hypothesis that defends how emotional aspects such as *motivation, self-confidence,* and *anxiety* can affect the second language acquisition process. Therefore, when the affective filter is high it means that the performer is probably unmotivated, not confident, or even anxious, which consequently leads to the blocking of the input, preventing it from accessing the language acquisition brain area. On the contrary, when there is motivation, confidence and the environment does not lead to anxiety, the affective filter lowers and the input is able to get in (*ibid.,* p. 81).

It is possible to identify some of the characteristics of both fields in the table below.

Bilingualism	Second language acquisition
The discipline that studies the ability to use two or more languages or dialects on a daily basis.	A discipline that studies the process of acquiring/learning another language after the native one has already been acquired/learned.
Classify types of bilinguals according to linguistic, developmental and social dimensions; evaluate the competence in language considering the languages as they are used in everyday life.	Describe and explain the learners' linguistic or communicative competence focusing on specific aspects of their performance.
Analysis of linguistic mode and its consequence on the bilingual language behavior.	Hypotheses aiming to answer how another than the first language is acquired.

SLA theory at its beginning sought to describe and explain the learners' language considering their performance, as well as their errors, whereas bilingualism focused on the comparison between the bilingual and the monolingual and how the languages one speaks (or not) interfere in his/her intelligence.

References

1. Baker C. (2001). *Foundations of Bilingual Education and Bilingualism*, 3rd edn. Multilingual Matters.

2. Butler, Y. G., & Hakuta, K. (2004). Bilingualism and second language acquisition. In Bhatia, T. & Ritchie, W. C. (Eds.), *The handbook of bilingualism* (pp. 114–144). Malden, MA: Blackwell.

3. Ellis, R. (1994). *The study of second language acquisition*. London: Oxford University Press.

4. Gass, S. (2013). *Second language acquisition*: An introductory course (4th ed.). New York, NY: Routledge.

5. Grosjean, F. (1997). The bilingual individual. *International Journal of Research and Practice in Interpreting*. 2:1-2, 163-187.

6. Grosjean, F. (2008). *Studying bilinguals*, Oxford, UK: Oxford University Press.

7. Krashen, S. D. (1982). *Principles and practice in second language acquisition*. Oxford: Pergamon Press.

8.   Krashen, S. D. (1985). *The input hypothesis: Issues and implications*. New York: Longman.

9.   Larsen-Freeman, D. (1991). Second Language Acquisition Research: Staking out the Territory. *TESOL Quarterly*, 25(2), 315–350. https://doi.org/10.2307/3587466

10.   Larsen-Freeman, D. (2000). Second Language Acquisition and Applied Linguistics. *Annual Review of Applied Linguistics*, *20*, 165-181. https://doi.org/10.1017/S026719050020010X.

11.   Liddicoat, A., ed. (1991). *Bilingualism: An Introduction*, Melbourne: Australian National Language Institute.

12.   Moradi, H. (2014). An investigation through different types of bilinguals and bilingualism. *International Journal of Humanities & Social Science Studies (IJHSSS)*. I (II), 107-112.

13.   Myers-Scotton, C. (2006). *Multiple voices*: An Introduction to bilingualism. Malden, MA: Blackwell.

14.   VanPatten, B., & Williams, J. (Eds.). (2014). *Theories in Second Language Acquisition*: An Introduction (2nd ed.). Routledge. https://doi.org/10.4324/9780203628942.

Authors' bio

The co-author of the same paper, **Anna Kellen Ribeiro Weng**, has presently been working as an EFL teacher in Brazil since 2017. She is primarily interested in Bilingualism and Second Language Acquisition. As an English teacher, her main focus has been on the teacher identity formation during the process of initial teaching education. She is graduated in English language and literature from the Mid Western State University, Brazil. Her central areas of concern comprise written diary, reports regarding her teaching experience.

Plinio Marco De Toni has presently been working as a professor in the department of psychology at MidWestern State University, Brazil. Besides, he is a psychologist with a master degree in child psychology. He is also doctorate in school psychology, with emphasis on development Neuro-psychology. In addition to it, he coordinates the psychology of Bilingualism where he is engaged in developing research studies in Billingualism, Psychology of Language Learning and family language policies. He is also acting as an instructor in billingualism and SLA in English as a medium of instruction. His research paper cover diverse fields of English language.

N. Lazebna / D. Kumar (Ed.), Studies in Modern English, Würzburg, 2022, p. 25-39. DOI: 10.25972/WUP-978-3-95826-199-0-25

The aphoristic potential of presidential rhetoric of G. Bush Jr.

Elina Kushch[*]

Abstract

This research paper concentrates on the analysis of the aphoristic potential of G. W. Bush's presidential rhetoric. Aphorisms are the most ancient laconic forms of expressing original and completed thoughts which reveal the peculiarity of their authors' world perception and worldview. From this perspective, these units can serve as the means of values codification. Repeatability and widespread use of aphorisms in various communications contribute to transmitting the values and ideas between the generations.

Political aphorisms, which are a combination of aphoristic expressions from political communication and discourse, play an important role in this process. The authors of these expressions are not only politicians, but also philosophers, historians, writers, celebrities of different nationalities and generations. Presidential rhetoric is an integral and significant part of political discourse.

The use of aphorisms as the means of codification of national and common human values in President G. W. Bush's formal addresses and speeches is intentional. It makes them concise and original, influential and convincing. Aphoristic expressions denoting common human values show the ideas and beliefs of their authors, as well as the politician, about life, justice, equality, freedom, faith, family. Aphorisms defining national values become the means of updating concepts of democracy, unity and diversity, freedom and security, success, and opportunity to fulfill one's potential in American society. The distinctive feature of G.W. Bush's rhetoric is the frequent use of aphorisms whose authors are the Founding Fathers.

Keywords: aphorism, common human values and national values, political discourse, presidential rhetoric.

For long, aphorisms have been attracting the attention of scientists from various fields of human sciences: literature studies, rhetoric, philosophy, paremiology, folklore studies, linguistics, intercultural communication, etc. The word 'aphorism' (from ancient Greek ἀφορισμός – *definition*) first appeared in the title of the treatise about the art of healing written by the ancient Greek physician, philosopher, and writer Hippocrates (460-370 B.C.). Because of this fact, Hippocrates is considered to be a founder and father of aphoristic discourse (Hui, 2019, p. 17), and his sententiae written in the Ionic dialect of ancient Greek are

---

[*] Associate Professor ,Theory and Practice of Translation Department, Zaporizhzhia Polytechnic National University, Zaporizhzhia, Ukraine.

often cited in Latin and translated into other world's languages, in particular: *noli nocere – do no harm* (basic physician's commandment stated by Hippocrates); *ars longa, vita brevis – art is long, life is short*; *Quae medicamenta non sanant, ferrum sanat; quae ferrum non sanat, ignis sana – with fire and sword* (rephrased "iron cures what drugs cannot, fire cures what iron cannot"); *contraria contrariis curantur – opposites are cured by opposites*; *omnium profecto artium medicina nobilissima – surely the Medicine is the noblest of all the arts.*

Aphorisms reflect the mentality of people from different countries and epochs, and representatives of different religious beliefs. 'They reflect not only opinions and standpoints of their authors stipulated by their ethnic culture but also bring up common human topics: specificity of the universe, society, life' (Kushch, Zankova, 2018, 290). An example of such aphorisms are the aphorisms of ancient Greek thinkers like Pythagoras, Democritus, Socrates, Plato, Aristotle, etc. The books of aphorisms were used for studying at schools in Old Greece. In the East, the aphoristic thought was, first of all, moral-oriented and defined by the ideal of self-enhancement. Confucius, Lao-Tze, and others played a big role in the development of Eastern aphoristic art.

Notwithstanding that the aphorisms appeared already in ancient times, their interpretation and understanding vary. Today, there are many definitions of the term 'aphorism' in scientific literature, including 'short wise phrase' (Kelvin, 2018, p. 127); 'short statement that says something wise and true' (Grant, 2016, p. 11); 'short pithy maxim' (Smith, 1998, p. 20); 'short witty sentence which expresses general truth or comment' (Zijderveld, 1979, p. 20); 'a concise expression of doctrine or principle, or any generally accepted truth conveyed in a pithy statement' (Peterson, 2017, p. 17).

American researcher J. Geary has formulated the main requirement to the aphorisms according to which they must be short, authoritative, philosophic, and original, contain original judgments and have an author (Geary, 2005, p. 32-33). The above-mentioned signs and features of the aphorisms were generalized by Russian linguist S.H. Vorkachev who suggested his definition of the aphorism: 'author's expression characterized by laconic and expressive form, completeness and generalization, and originality (sometimes paradoxical)' (Vorkachev, 2017, p. 14).

Aphorisms represent the values of their authors from different perspectives and in the most concentrated form and at the same time reflect their specific world perception and world views. Evaluating character of aphorisms is stipulated by their cumulative and influencing functions. On the one hand, aphorisms reflect author' side as of social or personal importance; on the other hand, aphorisms are used to affect the addressee due to authoritativeness of generalizations and assessments of an aphorism, preciosity and beauty of opinion expression.

Reproducibility of aphorisms contributes to transmitting the values from generation to generation. Political aphorisms are highly important in this transmitting. Having called the scope of aphorisms of the political discourse by the above-mentioned term, Russian researcher E. I. Sheigal considers such aphorisms as 'linguistic reflexes of political communication, a cultural trace which a political communication agent leaves when he uses expressions of famous political, historical, literary figures, which became popular and replicable after having been added to the precedent statements vocabulary of certain linguistic culture (Sheigal, 2000, p. 154). The above given definition proves that the scientist includes both aphoristic expressions created by the politicians and aphorisms of other authors which the politicians use into the concept of political aphorisms. Political aphorisms are a tool of codifying common human and national values.

Aphorisms denoting common human values and national values are integral components of George Walker Bush's presidential rhetoric. He was the President (from January 22, 2001 till January 20, 2009) in rather hard times for the country. After almost eight months after he started his presidentship (September 11, 2001) terrorist attacks were committed by the members of Islamic terrorist organization 'Al-Qaeda'. As a result of the terrorist attacks 2996 people were killed, more than 6000 people were injured, the World Trade Center and the surrounded buildings were collapsed in New York and that stopped the work in a considerable part of Lower Manhattan and caused $10 billion damages.

After tragic events of September 11, 2001, President G. W. Bush declared the global war against the terrorism. The USA sent troops to Afghanistan in 2001 and then to Iraq in 2003 to overthrow Saddam Hussein's regime. Although the problems of national danger were top priority for G. Bush, he also carried out some reforms in healthcare, education, social care, and reduced the taxes significantly as he had promised in his inauguration speech. On March 16, 2006, G. W. Bush unveiled the next national security strategy. It strengthened and developed the principles of domestic and foreign policy of the country. The core of these principles was in spreading the ideals of freedom, human rights with the aim of protecting American interests, neutralization of anti-American regimes, elimination of terrorist threat, and national security protection of the USA.

In December 2007, the worst crisis since World War II began and forced G. Bush and his administrations to interfere intensively in complicated economic issues of the country. Notwithstanding that, G. W. Bush's first-term ratings were very high and the majority of the country supported him, during the second term his ratings remarkably decreased. It was caused by several factors: difficult economic situation in the country; crisis which was caused by the most destructive in the history hurricane Katrina (August 2005); criticizing G. W. Bush's military actions and foreign policy towards some Oriental countries by a part of the US people.

Emotional intelligence and outstanding organizational abilities are not all characteristics and traits of this political figure, which helped him to become the President of the country and overcome the difficulties, which occurred in the country during his presidency. Despite the criticism, he is deemed to be a prominent and strong politician who 'is able to make counter-arguments, give a reason for his positions and convince the others in them' (Updegrove, 2017, p. 31).

G. W. Bush Jr's political speeches and addresses are characterized by expressiveness and originality; they speak for impulsivity and emotionality of his character, charisma of his speaking personality. The use of aphorisms in his official speeches and addresses contributed to their expressivity, figurativeness, persuasion, and influence since the aphorisms are the means of codifying common human and national values.

Common human values are called universal, core values (Borzenko, Kuvakin, Kudishina, 2002, p. 12). They reflect humanity interests; they are free from religious, political relationships and preferences. Common human values are a system where the basic elements are not only the moral principles, esthetical or law ideals, but also natural and social world with people and communities living in it. These values are not in born. They are im-planted during brining up. The values having been molded by values-based orientations, define the priority of social and cultural development of a personality and communities, and are fixated by social practice and life experience of an individual. The ultimate value is *a human life* which is a treasure for a human being and the background for all his other values (Kuznetsov, 1991, p. 24). That is why many philosophers, writers, academic research-ers, including American ones, made life an object of their aphorisms, for example: *You must live in the present, launch yourself on every wave, find your eternity in each moment* (Henry David Thoreau); *Life consists in what a man is thinking of all day*; (Ralph Waldo Emerson); *We cannot be sure what we have something to live for unless we are ready to die for it* (Eric Hoffer).

Common human values also display the ideas of humanism (Lat. *humanis* – human) which is a system of worldviews identifying a human life and protection of health, freedom, inherent worth, human right for happiness, development, and activity as a priority (Bor-zenko, Kuvakin, Kudishina, 2002, p. 12). The concept of humanism is also associated with humaneness and love for mankind (Kuznetsov, 1991). Humanism prevents appearance and spread of violence, cruelty and war, promotes peace and concord in communities.

Aphorisms denoting common human values were frequently used by G. W. Bush:

> We should save Social Security first, strengthen Medicare and expand it to cover life-saving prescription drugs, bring revolutionary improvements to our public schools, which will make us more competitive in the new century ahead; and enact the right kind of tax cuts for middle class families. **Life grants nothing to mortals without hard work. We can do this work together to improve** life of American people (Bush, 2011, p. 311).

This example is a fragment from George Bush's speech to the electorate in New Orleans, LA during the presidential race. Along with the phrases where the politician states what exactly he is going to do after he becomes the President, he uses aphorism *Life grants nothing to mortals without hard work*. The author of this aphorism is a famous ancient Roman poet Horace (65– 8 B.C.) whose works were written during the period of civil wars at the end of Roman Republic (509-27 B.C.) and beginning of reign of Augustus Octavian (31-14 B.C.), the founder of the Roman Empire. The aphorism reveals Horace's idea about the life of a common man and the place of work in it.

It is known that Horace's father wasn't rich. He was a freedman, which means a freed slave. Although, from a legal perspective the children of freedmen were equal to freeborn ones the Romans considered such origin socially invalid. This fact affected Horace's worldview and works. And the above-mentioned poet's aphorism reflects that.

The use of this aphorism enables George Bush to stress that he not only identifies himself as a common American who knows that kind of work, but is ready to work hard for the welfare of his home country and its people. The following sentence which the politician used in his speech is illustrative of the same ('*We can do this work together to improve life of American people*'). The use of aphoristic expression adds to influence, persuasiveness and authoritativeness of the politician's speech.

At the beginning of his work in the position of the President George W. Bush considered improving the economic level of living in the country, reducing taxes for its people, growth of profitable companies, more effective budget balancing as the top objectives. That is what he was talking about in his address the extract of which is given below:

> Economic improvement comes from the improved conditions of the whole population, not a small fraction. That's the formula today. And it works. We need to lift up all Americans, not just the wealthy few. You remember that justice cannot be for one side, but must be for both. We need to fight for all people, not just the well-connected and powerful. I've made my priorities clear, and they are the same priorities that brought us today's prosperity: balance the budget, pay down our debt, and invest in the best enterprise of all, the American people themselves. Put people first. Put their welfare first (Bush, 2011, p. 32).

In the above extract from the politician's discourse we can see the aphorism *justice cannot be for one side, but must be for both*. This aphorism belongs to Eleanor Roosevelt (1884-1962), American social activist, politician, and wife of the 32nd President of the USA (1933-1945), Franklin Roosevelt (1882-1945). She also was a niece of Theodore Roosevelt (1858-1919), the 26th President (1901-1909).

It is known that Eleonor Roosevelt's husband became the President at the difficult time of economic crisis in the USA (the Great Depression 1929-1939). His undisputed achievements are economic and social reforms which steered the country out of the economic crisis and at the same time made him popular among his countrymen. Theodore Roosevelt was the one who occupied the position of the President more than two terms (four terms). Despite uneasy relationships between the spouses, Eleonor always supported his husband, helped him with work working a lot for the benefit of the country.

The use of the aphorism whose author is one of the most popular first ladies of the country contributes to promoting ideas and suggestions provided in George W. Bush's discourse, attracts attention to his speech making him influential land convincing. The use of the above aphorism along with other sentences defining intentions and prioritized positions of his actions as a political figure shows that he presents himself as a fair politician willing to work for the welfare and assert the rights of every segment of the population independently of their material conditions. Also, we can see the use of aphorism as a tool of codifying common human values in another extract of politician's address:

> The teaching of our tradition is simple and permanent: 'love your neighbor as yourself'. Not just because this promotes the peace and good order of society. But because this is the proper way to treat human beings created in the image and likeness of God. We have these human characteristics in common. Every human being should be treated with dignity, respect, courtesy, fairness, and tolerance. No person should be subjugated or coerced or manipulated. Justice is the greatest distinguishing feature of democracy (Bush, 2011, p. 217).

In this extract of the politician's address devoted to acknowledgment of common human and national values in the country, he uses allusion '*love your neighbor as yourself*' which refers the addressee to the lines from the Bible (The Holy Bible, 2006, p. 311), and aphorism '*justice is the greatest distinguishing feature of democracy*' whose author is an American philosopher, one of the presidents of the University of Chicago, Robert Maynard Hutchins (1899-1945). Allusion is a 'concealed reference to certain historical, mythological, biblical, literature fact or daily-life fact' (Baldick, 2011, p. 12). The allusion used by George W. Bush

Jr in his speech shows what attitude a person should have towards others according to the law of God because the texts from Bible 'represent universal values related to ecology (generally speaking) of relations between the people, between man and the Creator, man and nature, the Creator and nature' (Zhyhareva, 2018, p. 46).

The aphorism used by the politician is a tool of declaring and explaining such values as justice and democracy. The use of the above-mentioned units makes the politician's speech more influential, expressive, convincing and authoritative, and draws attention to it.

In his the most essential political speeches, George Bush Jr. always used aphorisms which belong to 'the Founding Fathers of the USA', political figures who played the key role in the foundation and evolvement of American statehood, gaining independence and creating principles of its nationhood. American historians named seven politicians who had taken part in the most important processes of state formation (arranging and leading American revolution (1775-1783), proclaiming the independence (July 4, 1776) and creation of the Constitution (October17, 1778). These politicians are deemed the Founding Fathers of the USA: Benjamin Franklin (1706-1790), George Washington (1739-1799), John Adams (1735-1826), Thomas Paine (1737-1809), Thomas Jefferson (1743-1826), John Jay (1745-1829), James Madison (1751-1836), Alex Hamilton (1755-1804) (Kuklick, 2009, p. 32).

We see the use of aphorism in the fragment of his addressing speech in the early days of his presidency (January 24, 2001):

> Success, prosperity and strength of our nation is impossible without genuine, individual opportunity, without faith in the future, without a society based on trust and cooperation. **Trust starts with trustworthy leadership**. Establishing, growing and extending trust are my main tasks as a president (Bush, 2011, p. 69).

Addressing to his countrymen, George W. Bush points at the factors which determine success, prosperity and strength of American nation (*genuine, individual opportunity, without faith in the future, without a society based on trust and cooperation*). In addition to the above listed, the politician uses aphorism *trust starts with trustworthy leadership* the author of which is Benjamin Franklin (1706-1790), the famous American political figure, diplomat, writer, journalist, leader of War of Independence, and national hero.

As we know, Benjamin Franklin, a political figure, was the one who signed the main historical document which became the basis for the foundation of the USA as a separate state. The above-mentioned aphorism reveals the politician's opinion on what trust must start within the society. Obviously, Benjamin Franklin associated this concept with management and politics. This aphorism used by George W. Bush encourages the representatives of American nation to trust him and at the same time makes his speech more convincing, authoritative and influential.

The use of the aphorism which belongs to one of the Founding Fathers of the USA is present in another George W. Bush's speech:

> America at its best is a place where personal responsibility is valued and expected. **Encouraging responsibility is a call to conscience**. And though it requires sacrifice, it brings a deeper fulfillment. We find the fullness of life not only in options but in commitments. And we find that children and community are the commitments that set us free... God bless you all, and God bless America (Bush, 2011, p. 392).

In his speech, describing his country in the most positive way the President uses the aphorism encouraging responsibility is a call to conscience which belongs to another remarkable US politician, the 1st Vice President (1789-1797) and the 2nd President of the country (1797-1801),John Adams (1735-1826). John Adams was very conscientious, absolutely honest and responsible person (Kuklick, 2009, p. 36). The aphoristic expression givena bove shows his idea about the connection between such human virtues as responsibility and conscience.

President George W. Bush also used aphorisms whose authors were the Founding Fathers of the country in his felicitation speeches, for example:

> … Our nation was founded on a clear, simple and easily stated premise 'all men are created equal and they are endowed by their creator with certain unalienable rights…' This statement proves that equality and human rights don't come from the Constitution, laws passed by the Congress or decisions made by the Supreme Court. **Equality and human rights rest on the power and the will of Almighty God, not on a human foundation** (Bush, 2011, p. 359).

This example is a passage from the presidential speech delivered in 2003 on Thanksgiving Day (Thanksgiving Day) which is one of the oldest and the most loved holidays of Americans. Thanksgiving Day is annually celebrated in the country on the fourth Thursday of November. This day American families go to the church, and in the evening, they gather around the table. They serve a turkey with cranberry sauce, which is traditional for this holiday, and sweet pumpkin pie, sweet corn, apples, grape and other food and dishes, which symbolize the gifts of fall; people pray and give thanks to God and to each other for these gifts. The food pantries are opened all around the country this day, and on the eve, money, gifts, and food are distributed to the people in need.

The tradition of serving the turkey at the President's table exists in the country many years. More than 25 years the US presidents grant pardon to one or two turkeys intended for the presidential table. This day is a holiday of expressing thanks to God, family and friends for wellbeing and positive attitude towards them. The tradition of celebrating Thanksgiving Day traces to the foundation of America when the early pioneers arrived to the New World. Then, after severe winter with help of aboriginal people they learnt to till the land, grow pumpkin, corn, beans and gathered a good crop in fall 1621. So, they decided to express their gratitude to the God and invited the Indians who helped them to survive for the holiday.

Thanksgiving Day became a national holiday in 1789 thanks to the 1st President George Washington who delivered the official address to Americans giving thanks to God and his countrymen and showing respect to this tradition. Also, George Washington signed the decree on celebration of Thanksgiving Day on November 26 and since 1941 this holiday is celebrated every last Thursday of November. It should be noted that Thanksgiving Day is celebrated not only in the USA but also in Canada (annually on the first Monday of October) and it is deemed a common South American holiday.

Showing respect to ancestors' traditions and addressing to his countrymen on Thanksgiving Day on November 27, 2003, the President George Walker Bush used aphoristic phrase equality and human rights rest on the power and the will of Almighty God, not on a human foundation in his speech. The author of this expression is James Madison

(1751-1836), an outstanding American statesman, the 4th President (1809-1817) and one of the authors of the Constitution and Bill of Rights which confirmed the rights and freedoms of the citizens (1791).

The above specified aphorism reveals the politician's attitude to such common human values as equality and human rights. This aphorism used in George Bush's speech makes it more expressive and increase the effect on the addressee. The President Bush Jr. maintained the tradition of celebrating Thanksgiving Day not only by delivering speeches, giving presents to friends and family, but also by visiting military bases and dishing out meals to American soldiers.

Hurricane Katrina became a real hardship for American nation (August 23-31, 2005). The hurricane was the most destructive in the US history. As a result, 1836 people died and 80% of New Orleans, LA was underwater. The other states were hard hit too. More than 100,000 American families lost their homes. In America the hurricane caused $125 billion in economic damage.

Here is a citation from President George Bush Jr.'s speech given in New Orleans after hurricane Katrina (September 2005):

> Good evening. I am speaking to you from the city of New Orleans - nearly empty, still partly under water, and waiting for life and hope to return. Eastward from Lake Pontchartrain, across the Mississippi coast, to Alabama and into Florida, millions of lives were changed in a day by a cruel and wasteful storm…Hurricane Katrina is one of the strongest and destructive calamities we have ever had…
>
> Tonight so many victims of the hurricane and the flood are far from home and friends and familiar things. You need to know that our whole Nation cares about you - and in the journey ahead you are not alone. To all who carry a burden of loss, I extend the deepest sympathy of our country. To every person who has served and sacrificed in this emergency, I offer the gratitude of our country. And tonight I also offer this pledge of the American people: Throughout the area hit by the hurricane, we will do what it takes 'we will stay as long as it takes' to help citizens rebuild their communities and their lives. All who question the future of the Crescent City need to know: there is no way to imagine America without New Orleans, and this great city will rise again. Faith, discipline and self-sacrificing devotion help to overcome everything (Bush, 2011, p. 311).

In his speech the President not only focuses on devastating consequences of hurricane Katrina, but also extends his deepest sympathy for hurricane victims and their families and expresses gratitude for all people who are involved in restoring the life after destructive effect of the hurricane, supports the victims and helps them. Promising his help, the politician uses aphoristic expression *Faith, discipline and self-sacrificing devotion help to overcome everything*, where he lists the human virtues which help a person to overcome difficulties in his life. This aphorism is used by the politician in order to support and cheer up his countrymen. The author of this aphorism is a famous statesman and the 1st President, George Washington (1732-1799).

George W. Bush considered family to be one of the key values of every person's life and American society in general:

In this world of change, some things do not change: the values we try to live by, the institutions that give our lives meaning and purpose. Our society rests on a foundation of responsibility and family commitment. **The family is link to our past and bridge to our future.** Family supports and gives us strength. Family helps us to cope with problems and overcome difficulties. The role of family cannot be overestimated. This fundamental institution links every individual to a society and performs the mediating function in it (Bush, 2011, p. 301).

Pointing out the role of family in every person's life and in American society in general, the politician uses aphorism *the family is link to our past and bridge to our future,* which belong to American writer Alex Haley (1921-1992). The writer became famous due to his autobiographical novel '*Roots: The Saga of an American Family*' where he told the story of his family that traced back to African ancestors. The novel was published in 1976 and became popular immediately. It was translated into 37 languages and a television miniseries was filmed based on its plot, and the author received a Pulitzer Prize award (in 1977) for his novel. The aphorism reveals the politician's idea about the key role of family in connecting the generations. The use of this aphorism draws attention to President George W. Bush's speech and makes it more influential and authoritative.

Distinctive and unique character of American national values are based on their history, system of views and ideas in social, political, economic, cultural and others aspects of life. National values are determined by the mindset of Americans. D. DeVos, an American philosopher, determined the basic values-based orientations of his nation: freedom, democracy, private property, equality of opportunity, individualism (DeVos, 1997, p. 31-34). American values also include pragmatism, activity, hard work, pro-activity, self-confidence (Razorenov, 2012, p. 505).

In his speeches, George W. Bush also used quite a lot of aphorisms to denote the national values in American community. He appeals to these values, first of all, in the most important his speeches addressed to his countrymen and the whole world. One of such speeches is the presidential address to nation on September11, 2001. The extract of this speech is given below:

Good evening. Today, our fellow citizens, our way of life, our very freedom came under attack in a series of deliberate and deadly terrorist acts. The victims were in airplanes, or in their offices; secretaries, businessmen and women, military and federal workers; moms and dads, friends and neighbors. Thousands of lives were suddenly ended by evil, despicable acts of terror...
America and our friends and allies join with all those who want peace and security in the world, and we stand together to win the war against terrorism. Tonight, I ask for your prayers for all those who grieve, for the children whose worlds have been shattered, for all whose sense of safety and security has been threatened. **The safety of the people is the highest law**. And I pray they will be comforted by a power greater than any of us, spoken through the ages in Psalm 23:4 'Even though I walk through the valley of the shadow of death, I fear no evil, for You are with me.'
This is a day when all Americans from every walk of life unite in our resolve for justice and peace. America has stood down enemies before, and we will do so this time. None

of us will ever forget this day. Yet, we go forward to defend freedom and all that is good and just in our world.
Thank you. Good night and God bless America (Bush, 2011, p. 26).

Addressing to the representatives of American nation, the President of the country acknowledges the horror of consequences of the terrorist attacks (*The victims were in airplanes, or in their offices; secretaries, businessmen and women, military and federal workers; moms and dads, friends and neighbors. Thousands of lives were suddenly ended by evil, despicable acts of terror*) and stresses that not only American nation, but friends and alliance partners of the country have united in struggle against the terrorism giving their support to the USA (*America and our friends and allies join with all those who want peace and security in the world, and we stand together to win the war against terrorism*). Calling his countrymen for praying for innocent victims the politician uses aphorism *the safety of the people is the highest law* which displays his view on importance of human and community security. This aphorism belongs to Cicero (106-43 B.C.), a famous ancient Roman political figure, orator and philosopher whose works are deemed the most important sources of knowledge about life in Rome in 1st century B.C. In politician's speech, calling for prays goes along with the lines from the Psalms of the Old Testament where it is said that with God's help a man should not afraid of evil (*Even though I walk through the valley of the shadow of death, I fear no evil, for You are with me*). In the politician's speech, the psalm was slightly reworded comparing to the version in the Bible (*Even though I walk through the darkest valley, I will fear no evil, for you are with me*) (The Holy Bible, 2006,p. 317). The use of the above-mentioned lines from the Bible adds to expressivity of the politician's speech and enables him to note that God hasn't left his nation and will support it.

Let's analyze the extract of another George W. Bush's speech devoted to the tragic events of September 11, 2001:

A great writer has said that **the struggle of humanity against tyranny is the struggle of memory against forgetting**. When we fight terror, we fight tyranny; and so we remember. We remember the perfect blueness of the sky that Tuesday morning. We remember the children traveling without their mothers when their planes were hijacked.
We remember the cruelty of the murderers and the pain and anguish of the murdered. Every one of the innocents who died on September the 11th was the most important person on earth to somebody. Every death extinguished a world...
In time, perhaps, we will mark the memory of September the 11th in stone and metal – something we can show children as yet unborn to help them understand what happened on this minute and on this day.
But for those of us who lived through these events, the only marker we'll ever need is the tick of a clock at the 46th minute of the eighth hour of the 11th day. We will remember where we were and how we felt. We will remember the dead and what we owe them. We will remember what we lost and what we found. And in our time, we will honor the memory of the 11th day by doing our duty as citizens of this great country, freedom's home and freedoms defender. And **those who deny freedom to others deserve it not for themselves**. God bless (Bush, 2011, p. 202).

This extract from the discourse is a part of President G. W. Bush's solemn speech 'The World Will Always Remember September 11' which he delivered in the White House three months after the tragic events of 9/11 (December 11, 2001). The politician's speech begins with aphorism of Milan Kundera (born in 1929), a famous French writer of Czech origin, *the struggle of humanity against tyranny is the struggle of memory against forgetting.* The use of this phrase by the political figure at the beginning of his speech is emblematic because it is aimed at stressing the necessity of struggle against tyranny and terrorism, and remembrance of the tragic events that led to deaths and other terrifying consequences in the country.

G. W. Bush's speech contains aphoristic phrase *And those who deny freedom to others, deserve it not for themselves,* which belongs to Abraham Lincoln (1809-1865), an American nation hero, the 16th President. This politician is one of the key figures in the history of the USA. It is deemed that he was the one who prevented the country from breaking up, greatly contributed to economic growth of the country, helped forward the abolition which was the main obstacle to normal evolution of the country. He also formulated the principles of democratic government '*The government of the people, by the people, for the people*' (cit. from Kuklick, 2009, p. 34).

Abraham Lincoln was the 1st President, and he was fatally wounded (April 4, 1865). After his assassination, the economy of the USA started to grow intensively, which helped the country become the global leader in the early 21st century. He is considered to be one of the most intellectual and loved presidents of the country. As gratitude from American nation, a memorial (1922) symbolizing president's belief that all people must be free was built. The use of Abraham Lincoln's aphorism by President Bush at the end of his speech is not accidental. Thanks to it G. W. Bush stresses that he espouses the ideas and principles of development of democratic and free society which were implemented by his ancestors, and stipulates what is waiting for those who violate safety and freedom of this country. The use of these aphoristic phrases makes his speech more expressive, solemn and powerful.

We can see the use of aphorism aiming to codify the value of freedom in G. W. Bush's inaugural address the passage of which is below:

> Thank you, all. Chief Justice Rehnquist, President Carter, President Bush, President Clinton, distinguished guests, and my fellow citizens. The peaceful transfer of authority is rare in history, yet common in our country. With a simple oath, we affirm old traditions and make new beginnings.
>
> As I begin, I thank President Clinton for his service to our Nation, and I thank Vice President Gore for a contest conducted with spirit and ended with grace.
>
> I am honored and humbled to stand here where so many of America's leaders have come before me, and so many will follow. We have a place, all of us, in a long story, a story we continue but whose end we will not see. It is a story of a new world that became a friend and liberator of the old, the story of a slaveholding society that became a servant of freedom, the story of a power that went into the world to protect but not possess, to defend but not to conquer...
>
> Our unity, our Union, is a serious work of leaders and citizens and every generation. And this is my solemn pledge: I will work to build a single nation of justice and opportunity. I know this is in our reach because we are guided by a power larger than ourselves, who creates us equal, in His image, and we are confident in principles that unite and lead us onward. **The God who gave us life gave us liberty at the same time...**(Bush, 2011, p. 298).

In this passage of his inaugural address, G. W. Bush uses aphorism *the God who gave us life gave us liberty at the same time* whose author is Thomas Jefferson, one of the Founding Fathers of the USA. This aphorism illustrates that both politicians believe that the origin of their nation is divine, and God bequeathed liberty to the nation.

It is clear from the address that President G. W. Bush appeals to God and biblical themes not only in the above mentioned aphorism but also in the sentence *when we see that wounded traveller on the road to Jericho, we will not pass to the other side* where he uses the name of Jericho which is one of the holy cities of the Land of the Covenant. According to the Old Testament, after Moses' death God commanded Joshua the Son of Nun to lead the part of Jewish people, cross the river Jordan together, take the city of Jericho, and settle there and in its surroundings. The politician's address ends with sentence *God bless you all, and God bless America.*

Declaration of national values is also present in another G. W. Bush's solemn speech:

> We don't declare our diversity – we're united by it. We don't proclaim democracy – we live according to its principles. We don't just talk about our material wealth – we create it. We don't insist on any opportunity given by our country and its society because we know that America itself is another name for opportunity (Bush, 2011, p. 51).

The President represents American values (*diversity, democracy, material wealth, opportunity)* in a special manner. He speaks about them as if Americans not only declare, proclaim, etc. these values (*we don't declare...; we don't proclaim...; we don't just talk...; we don't insist ...*), but live according to these values or create them (*we're united by, we live according to, we create*).

We should draw attention to the use of aphoristic expression *America itself is another name for opportunity* in the politician's speech as it reveals both politician's and author's belief that America is a country of opportunity for people. The author of this aphorism is Ralph Emerson (1803-1882), a famous American writer and poet, pastor, philosopher and social activist. Using this phrase, in fact, G. W. Bush points to the opportunity to achieve American Dream, in particular opportunity for every man to fulfill his potential and achieve success in American society.

The concept of American Dream was formulated by the Founding Fathers of the USA and it was meant as 'an ideal of freedom and opportunity existed in the country' (cit. from Kuklick, 2009, p. 33). This word combination first appeared in historical treatise 'The Epic of America', 1931,written in the period of the Great Depression by James Adams (1878-1949), an American writer and historian: '*American dream is about land in which life should be better and richer and fuller for every man with opportunities for each according to ability or achievement*' (cit. from Kuklick, 2009, p. 34). This treatise was written by the author with purpose of supporting and cheering up his countrymen, reminding them of America's destiny and its great achievements. The concept of 'American Dream' traces its roots to the key historical document of the country, United States Declaration of Independence, 1776, where the British colonies of North America proclaimed themselves independent from the Great Britain. That was the document where the equality of all people and their rights to life, freedom, and happiness were confirmed.

Thus, the aphorisms reflect value-based ideas, guidelines and orientations of their authors. That is why these elements can be the means of denoting the values and explaining author's interpretation of these values. Political aphorisms have an essential role in this process. The notion of political aphorisms include aphorisms whose authors are not only political figures, but philosophers, writers, etc. Such people have no relation to politics, and are not involved in political activities; however, their aphorisms are used in political discourse. Political discourse, which is a type of institutional discourse, identifies the participants of political communication, and is defined by the subject of political communication. Political rhetoric plays the key role in it.

One of the contexts, where the aphorisms are used to denote common human and national values, is the political discourse of G. W. Bush, the 43th President of the USA. Common human values are associated with the ideas of humanism and mean the acknowledgment of priority of a human life and human life protection, freedom, human self-worth, right to happiness, enhancement, activity, etc. In politician's speeches, the objects of aphorisms were such common human values as life, justice, equality, liberty, faith, family. George Walker Bush's political discourse is also the context for use of aphorisms denoting such American values as democracy, unity and national diversity, freedom and security, success and opportunity to fulfill one's potential in society. The use of aphorisms in the politician's addresses contributed to their expressivity, authoritativeness, persuasiveness and influence.

In his key speeches and the most important addresses the politician used the aphorisms which belong to the Founding Fathers of the USA (Benjamin Franklin, George Washington, John Adams, Thomas Paine, Thomas Jefferson, John Jay, James Madison, and Alexander Hamilton) to denote common human and national values. The use of these aphorisms let George Walker Bush implicitly state that he embraces and spreads the leading ideas, thoughts and viewpoints of his famous countrymen and, at the same time, continues to serve their great cause. We see further perspectives for research in studying the aphorisms used by other Presidents of the USA in 20-21 centuries and the aphoristic potential of presidential rhetoric of other English-speaking countries of the world.

References

1. Baldick, C. (2001). The Concise Oxford Dictionary of Literary Terms. Oxford: Oxford University Press.

2. Borzenko, I. M., Kuvakin, V. A, Kudishina, A. A. (2020). Osnovy ovremennogo gumanizma: uchebnoje posobije dlya vuzov [Basis of modern humanism: teaching guide for universities] Moskwa: RGO.

3. Bush, W. G. (2011) Selected Speeches of President George W. Bush 2001-2008. Washington: U. S. Government.

4. DeVos, D. (1997). Rediscovering American Values: The Foundations of Our Freedom for the 21st century. New York: Penguin Group (USA) Incorporation.

5.   Geary, J. (2005). The World in a Phrase: A History of Aphorisms. London: Blooms-
      bury Publishing.

6.   Grant, B. (2016). The Aphorism and Other Short Forms (The New Critical Idiom).
      London: Routledge.

7.   Hippocrates, Verhoofd, L. (2015). The Aphorisms of Hippocrates. London: Andesite
      Press.

8.   Hui, A. (2019). A Theory of the Aphorism: From Confucius to Twitter. Princeton:
      Princeton University Press.

9.   Kelvin, R. (2018). Aphorisms: Gifted One-Liners. London: Austin MacAuley.

10.   Kuklick, B. (2009). A Political History of the USA: One Nation Under God. London:
      Palgrave Macmillan.

11.   Kushch, E. O., Zankova D. (2018). Lingvalniy status anglomovnogo aforyzmu [Lin-
      gual status of English-language aphorism]. *Naukovi zapyski. Serija 'Filologichni
      nauky'*. Vypusk 164. Kropyvnytzkyi: Vydavnytstvo «Kod».

12.   Kuznetsov, V. G. (1991). Obshchetselovechiskie tsennosti i ih soderganie [Universal
      human values and their content]. Moskwa: Izdatelstvo Moskovskogo universtiteta.

13.   Peterson, J. (2017). In Praise of Phrases. London: Edward Arnold.

14.   Razorenov, D. A. (2012). Systema tsennostey i antitsennostey v amerikanskom
      politicheskom soznanii [The system of values and antivalues in American political
      consciouss]. *Izvestija Tulskogo gosudarstvennogo universiteta*. Tula: Izdatelstvo
      Tulskogo gosudarstvennogo universiteta.

15.   Sheigal, E. I. (2000). Semiotika politicheskogo diskursa. Volgograd: Peremena.

16.   Smith, L. (1998). A Treasury of English Aphorisms. London: Palgrave.

17.   Stephanson, A. (1995). Manifest Destiny: American Expansionism and the Empire
      of Right. New York: Hill and Wang.

18.   Teague, G., Beechey, A. (2013). USA-Culture Smart!: The Essential Guide to Cus-
      toms & Culture. London: Kuperaed.

19.   The Holy Bible: King James Version (2006). Peabody, Massachusets: Hendrickson
      Publishers Inc.

20.   Updegrove, M. K. (2017). The Last Republicans: Inside the Extraordinary Relation-
      ship Between George H.W. Bush and George W. Bush. New York: Harper.

21.   Vorkachev, S. G. (2017). Lumen natural: aksiologija intellekta v jazyke: monografija
      [Lumen natural: axiology of intellect in the language: monograph]. Moskwa:
      FLINTA.

22.   Woods, H. F. (2013). American Sayings – Famous Phrases, Slogans and Aphorisms. Boston: Woods Press.

23.   Zhyhareva, O. O. (2018). Anglomovnyibibliyniy ekodiskurs u lingvopoetologich-nomu vysvitlenni: prostory pobudovy [English-language biblical ecodiscourse in linguopoetic interpretation: areas ofevolution]. Doctor's thesis. Kyiv Lingustic National University.

24.   Zijderveld, A. (1979). On Cliches and Witty Phrases. London: Routledge and Kegan Paul Ltd.

Author's bio

Elina Kushch, PhD in Philology, Associate Professor at the Department of Translation, Zaporizhzhia Polytechnic National University, Ukraine. E. Kushch was born in Zaporizhzhya, Ukraine on 28 March, 1975. In 2001 graduated from Kyiv State Linguistic University, Kyiv, Ukraine and got a Diploma of Teacher of English Language and Literature. She was a teacher of English at Zaporizhzhya Technical State University, Ukraine; a post-graduate student at Kyiv State Linguistic University, Ukraine; Associate Professor at National University "Zaporiz'ka Politechnika", 64, Zhukovskogo Street, National University "Zaporiz'ka Politechnika", Zaporizhzya, Ukraine. The areas of scientific interest: political linguistics, discourse analysis, lexical semantics, terminology, translation studies. As. Prof. Kushch has been the author of 115 articles published in local and international journals Kizil, M., Kushch, E. (2019). Thematic progression in English literary and legislative texts. Advanced Education, 12; Zhykharieva, O, Kushch, E. Stavtseva, V. (2021). Suggestive potential of Franklin D. Roosevelt's presidential speech 'Annual Address to the USA Congress'. Amazonia Investiga, 10 (37) as well as a monograph Varieties of English (2021) and a textbook Translation of English and Ukrainian Industry Specific Texts (2019). As. Prof. Kushch is a member of Ukrainian Association of Cognitive Linguistics and Poetics (UACLiP).

N. Lazebna / D. Kumar (Ed.), Studies in Modern English, Würzburg, 2022, p. 41-51. DOI: 10.25972/WUP-978-3-95826-199-0-41

English-language Digital Discourse of Human-Machine Communication

Nataliia Lazebna,[*] Anatoliy Prykhodko[†]

Abstract

The paper focuses on digital discourse. This is a speech-intellectual product of innovative information technologies, a phenomenon, which needs further interdisciplinary and linguistic interpretation. The English-language digital discourse shows how linguistic verbal communication is mediated by digits and to what extent these Signum and Verbum unity reigns over the world.

The paper analyzes the ways and methods of integrated and differential use of verbal and non-verbal sign systems in the English language as compared to programming languages, considering the types of synchronous changes in the socio-cultural dimension of the sign. This research describes the processes of signs transformation during their functioning in programming languages and in the English language, common and distinctive features in the arrangement of grammatical, lexical-semantic, and graphic means of (natural) English and (artificial) programming languages in their projection on different modes of communication in the system Human ↔ Machine.

Programming languages are constituted by verbal means of the English language with additional use of its own semiotic resources, which testifies to their integrative linguistic and mathematical nature. The specific representation of ElDD conveys its reciprocal nature when the English language using its own tools combines them with the elements of the programming languages thus creating an effective toolkit for self-processing.

Keywords: English-language digital discourse, linguistics, semiotics, digit, text processing, programming languages.

The scientific and technological progress of modernity disturbs the monopoly of natural language related to human communication, developing and contrasting it with programming languages. The linguistic dualism «natural language – artificial/synthetic language» is today an inherent feature of the information society, which begins to form the «machine picture of the world» (Jokuza, 2017, EP). English-language digital discourse (ElDD) outlines a new status of a Human in the form of «intermediate existence» between the real and virtual worlds. The phenomena of «naturalness» and «artificiality» are interrelated and in the

---

[*]   Privat Dozent, Dr. Habil., TEFL Methodology Department, Julius-Maximilians University of Wuerzburg, Wuerzburg, Germany.
[†]   Full Professor, Dr. Habil., Chair of Translation Theory and Practice Department, Zaporizhzhia National Polytechnic University, Zaporizhzhia, Ukraine.

context of studied discourse are harmoniously intertwined. The above mentioned pre-requisites of the research create an innovative basis for new linguistic development, digital linguistics, with ElDD as the central concept. ElDD is represented as a three-layer cognitive and communicative construct in the unity of micro-, meso-, and macro levels used for Human-Machine communication.

The Empirical Material is represented by English-language texts and text fragments, which relate to the existence of ElDD. The first part comprises texts in the English language, which are used in programming languages, for example, Python guidelines with examples [2012-2020], Scratch guidelines [2008-2010; 2020], and Squeak by Example 5.3 [2010-2020]. The second part includes texts used in innovative technologies focusing on texts describing natural language processing Multi-Domain Wizard-of-Oz dataset, NPS Chat Corpus, Stanford Question Answering Dataset (SQUAD). The third part comprises texts, which reflect the use of technologies for language processing (Github.com – scripts and answers of chatbots Alice, Eliza, Mitsuku, Rose).

Methods:

- interdisciplinary method is implemented to consider ElDD in different fields of science;
- descriptive methods to interpret and generalize basic practices of modern discursive studies;
- semiotic analysis to parametrize linguistic relevant properties of programming languages and natural language;
- linguo-cognitive analysis focuses on communication triggers between Human and Machine;
- discursive-textual analysis focuses on ElDD specifics and different levels of textual representation;
- functional-communicative method to analyze grammatical, textual, and graphic properties;
- structural modeling is used to grammatically describe the processes for clusterization, templates, and tokenization of ElDD textual space.

General Discussion

Pathos and mystery of human communication are broken by a third party, a digit, which becomes a kind of «superstructure». The natural language is specific and flexible because it quickly adapts to the laws of information technology and thus appears both as a primary system, a donor of discourse, and as a secondary modeling system or a focal point for creating artificial languages. ElDD is embodied as a powerful linguistic, social and cultural phenomenon (Lazebna, Prykhodko, 2021, EP).

ElDD, at the same time, is a kind of institutional communication mediated by a symbiosis of (artificial) programming languages and (natural) English language, which reflects the digitized speech act motivating verbal interaction of its agents and its clients by means of innovative information technologies. This studied type of discourse is an ideal self-generating system. Its linguistic and semiotic dominants focus on coding and decoding commands both aversively (from Human to Machine) and reversibly (Machine to Human). In this way, there is a reciprocal interaction between the target sphere of discourse (natural English) and the source-sphere (programming languages).

String»lineCount
"Answer the number of lines represented by the receiver, where every cr adds one line".
/cr count/
Cr :=Character cr.
count:= 1 min: self size.
self do:
[:c / c == cr ifTrue: [count := +1]] (Squeak, 2021, EP).

Fig. 1. Python language of programming

Figure 1 illustrates phonetic, lexical, and grammatical relations, which are transformed into a kind of linguistic and mathematical symbiosis, which is successfully used by discourse participants, its agents, and clients.

Participants of ElDD communicate within the appropriate text space, filled with digitized texts of clearly structured composition, certain cognitive-semantic reflections, and specific pragmatic guidelines that require appropriate competence. Textual representations of ElDD are a kind of intellectual products of participants' mental and speech activities in at least three registers of communication («Human–Human», «Human–Machine», «Human– Machine– Human – Human») and their variations, depending on the modes of direct or indirect communication, as well as the mode of their encoding and decoding.

For example, an abstract from the programming language Squeak highlights two modes of interaction «Human User – Human Programmer – Machine – Human User», where the User is looking for an explanation of the programming language functioning:

1) **FAQ 5** The browser does not look like the one described in the book. What gives? **Answer** You are probably using an image in which the OmniBrowser is installed as the default System browser. You can change the default by clicking on the little menu icon in the top-left corner of the browser window, between the «X» and the browser label, and selecting «Choose new default browser» from the menu that appears. Select #Browser to get the plain old browser. (This preference changes the effect of the World ◁ open . . . ◁ system browser menu, but not what happens when you drag the Browser icon from the Tools flap.) (RecipeQA, 2019, EP).

2) **FAQ 10** How do I tell which methods of a class are abstract? Answer abstract Methods := [:a Class | a Class method Dict keys select: [:a Method | (a Class>>a Method) is Abstract]]. Abstract Methods value: Collection – → an Identity Set (#remove: if Absent: #add: #do:).

In the first example (1) the author of the guideline explains the functionality of the programming language Squeak, using means of the natural language and only rarely built-in commands, symbols, and signs. In the second abstract the author appeals for the commands of the programming language Squeak.

The interaction «Human↔Machine» will be effective when the sender achieves his goal and the recipient meets the needs of the sender, but it does not always work, because the effectiveness of this interaction depends largely on the Machine. By changing voice commands, or making some phonetic or typographical errors in a search engine (such as Google), the Machine either modifies or cannot process the sent command / request, because the coded nature of the Machine depends on the dynamic and changing nature of Human (Makhachashvilli, Semenist, Zatsnyi, Klymenko, 2021, p. 148). That is why, it is impossible to modify and improve the acts of communication between Human and Machine, focusing exclusively on linguistic and mathematical procedures. Here, it will be necessary to re-deploy the interaction «Human –Machine»and turn it into a relationship «Client ↔ Programmer ↔ Machine ↔ Human»/ «Human-1 ↔ Human-2 ↔ Machine ↔ Human-1» / «Human-1 ↔ Human in Machine».

Whatever register of discursive communication between Human and Machine is considered, it will always produce the text as an output. The text space of English-language digital discourse has a three-layer structure, which consists of macro-, meso- and micro-levels.

Structure of horizontal contexts of ElDD

Texts of macro level			
Layer 1	Layer 2	Layer 3	
Verbal reflection of the information register	Meaning	Image	Horizontal context, commentary, hyperlink, navigation buttons
Texts of meso level			
Verbal/nonverbal reflection of the information register	Meaning	Code Tag	Vertical context, hyperlink
Texts of micro level			
Verbal reflection of the information register	Meaning	Image	Vertical context

Table 1. Structure of horizontal contexts of ElDD

The *microlevel of ElDD* is based on the texts of programming languages, lists of commands, and written programs having a mathematical basis with its set of digits and symbols. On the one hand, programming languages have the status of artificial ones, as they are chains of predications and written commands, and, on the other hand, they are a powerful tool for constructing digital discourse. In interaction with natural language, they form the inner linguistic- semiotic contour of English-language digital discourse.

The emergence of programming languages as a kind of «unified digitality» based on natural languages was a radical breakthrough in the movement of Human to artificial intelligence and opened new opportunities for communication with the Machine. On the one hand, the English language appears in this system as the primary donor system of programming languages, in particular, and digital discourse in general, and on the other hand, represents the secondary modeling systems that create artificial languages. In this context, the English language develops human-coded world and its fragments (Black et al., 2020, p. 223).

The most common programming languages based on the English language are Squeak, Scratch and Python. They create the internal contour of ElDD and have no oral channel for transmitting information, these languages are interconnected by global compositional determinism at the algorithmic level. Their differential feature is the lack of a common domain of interpretation between programs written in the natural (English) language. Most of them are characterized by local variables, systematic indexing, recursiveness, and lack of semantics without syntax.

Linguo-semiotic elements of micro level produce networks of relationships in which each of these elements in the context of programming languages or natural (English) language can be regenerated from a word or symbol into a command or query. For example:

```
# Define the sentence to be lemmatized
sentence = "The striped bats are hanging on their feet for best"
# Tokenize: Split the sentence into words
word_list = nltk.word_tokenize(sentence)
print(word_list)
#> ['The', 'striped', 'bats', 'are', 'hanging', 'on', 'their', 'feet', 'for', 'best']
# Lemmatize list of words and join
lemmatized_output = ' '.join([lemmatizer.lemmatize(w) for w in word_list])
print(lemmatized_output) (Scratch, 2021, EP).
```

In programming languages, communication is mediated by both machine and software codes. Therefore, visually (in the sign-symbolic version) you can see only a part of the information technology, i.e. the external form and user interface. In this case, the system of open-source code, algorithms, and structured representation of databases, technologies, techniques, and interfaces enables effective communication between Human and Machine (Gee, 2014, p. 134-147).

Texts created on the basis of programming languages show the clarity of their natural language form, differ in the nature of the prescribed commands and operational order. Further, these texts penetrate into the fabric of natural language and are embodied in the digital discursive environment mainly focusing on the use of a certain sequence of elements. These include lists, lines, tuples, and elements of the dictionary. They are all grouped around the idea of variability, the immutability of data, and orderliness/disorder of elements. In general, the textual representation of the micro-level of ElDD is characterized by structure, coherence, cohesion, the logic of construction and representation, as well as a symbiosis of natural language and (sub) language of mathematics (Gabbrielli, 2010, ER; Herring, 2004, p. 316).

The meso level of ElDD is the center of direct interaction of natural English and artificial programming languages. At this level, the former, using its own tools, integrates them with the elements of the latter, creating effective tools for processing «itself». Initially, the natural English language builds up the «bricks» for the development of analytical tools (creation of chatbots, natural language processing programs, NLTK, etc.), and as a result, the English language itself becomes the object of processing. In this way, the natural English language is regenerated in a technocratic and digitalized space.

The leading morphological categories most involved in the interaction of English and programming languages are auto-semantic units, which are, first of all, noun and verb. A nominative phrase with a noun at its top has a wide functional range for the transfer of information from the Machine to Human and vice versa. The nominative focus of ElDD participants initiates the activities of Human in cyberspace (creating requests for the Machine, searching for information in the network, verbalization of commands of programming languages, etc.). In combination with the verb, which is the vehicle for the categorical meaning, the effectiveness of information transfer increases many times. The verb appears in this system as a key representative of the message template, mediating the so-called agent focus. The agent focus of programming languages «migrates» from the ascertaining to the restrictive, not limited to the given semiotic framework (symbols, marks, tags). Within agent focus, commands of programming languages can be split into different constructs of alteration, creation, establishment, and obtaining. For example: *create_ package, generate_statement, start_listening* etc.

Morphological «awareness» of Human and Machine plays an important role at the meso- level of the analyzed discourse. It conveys the mastery of the mechanisms, which break tokens into morphs, which in the process of communication helps to «distill» the information transferred to the machine (Farhadi, 2015, p. 187). Morpho split is a process and, at the same time, the result of the «distillation» of morphs in the process of communication. Due to its digital nature, the morpho split becomes an important prerequisite for text clustering. The machine proceeds to the clustering of textual matter, triggering the morpho split. At the same time, it relies on a huge sample, turns to previous developments and vector representation of words, and involves tokenization, purification, and stemming to remove «noise» signs and symbols. For example, there are possibilities of active request representation (*classification, elaboration, research, treatment*):

Human: *Can you block my debit card?* Machine: *You're all set, your card is now locked. You can unlock it anytime with my help or in the app.*

Another option is to **represent characteristics of the request subject** (*attitude, consideration, discussion, reason, sense, availability, complexity, feature, order, reaction*): Machine: *Hello. How may I help you?* Human: *Hey, I lost my access.*

In ElDD there is also a description of request (*brief description, explanation, presentation*). Machine: *Here's the sweatshirt. Click below if you want more info, if you want more info or buy it.*

For the Machine as an agent of the meso-level development, grammatical categories of natural (English) language are transmitted using digital identifiers (gender, digit, time, etc.) Two important aspects of the interaction between natural and programming languages are temporality and modality (Van Leeuwen, 2011, p. 688).

In the case of text processing by means of the English language, the machine clearly follows the established algorithm: text → random separation (cleaning) of lexical units → ordering lexical units by parts of speech → digitization of lexical units (digitization). In the process of natural language processing, which is both an object and a tool of analysis, there is a need to algorithmize the mechanisms of machine word processing. Purification strategies become very effective: representation of the request, description of the request, means of information transfer, etc. In this process, the role of the Machine becomes exclusively instrumental: it performs its analytical function according to the criterion of words used. Ambivalence, synonymy, homonymy, and polysemy become interfering factors in the process of natural language processing by the Machine.

At the macro-level (external linguistic and semiotic contour) of its representation, ElDD creates the environment, mode, and style of sharing natural English by Human and Machine to establish mutually beneficial communication by producing structurally integrated, meaningfully relevant, and pragmatically targeted speech messages (Lazebna, 2021, p. 175). The mediator of such communication is a chatbot, an artificially created program that simulates interactions/conversation/dialogue with the User. The chatbot is gradually becoming a universal mediator in Human↔Machine communication. A chatbot is a certain «anthropomorphized» entity, created by a programmer, and is not just some digitalized entity, but something «humanlike». Chatbots range from animated interface agents, conversational agent and avatar. In terms of ElDD, the Machine can be both an author and interlocutor. A User interacts with the Machine to meet personal needs, avoid feelings of loneliness, search for information, and so on. The effectiveness of chatbots mediated by means of natural language is supported by introductory framing, special triggers, templates, and techniques for eliminating syntactic and semantic ambivalence. Chatbots involve a certain tactical and strategic arsenal, such as return, clarification, paraphrasing, reorientation, and so on (Yan, Duan, Bao, 2016, EP).

When the User communicates with an animated conversational agent, the model of living / natural speech is reproduced. Its successful pre-requisite is the operational linguistics of discourse, the logic of using appropriate elements of programming language, the efficiency of the Machine response, and most importantly, the response of the «Machine» to «Human». Similar to natural communication, such speech exchange involves a rhythmic alteration of the communicative roles of the sender and the recipient, the client and the agent of the discourse.

The communicative and functional potential of discourse plays an important role in the management of human and machine speech exchange, which involves the harmonious use of compositional and architectonic-speech forms, speech and discursive acts, maxims of cooperation, and politeness. With the proximity of natural («human») communication, the macro-level of ElDD actively uses established architectonic-speech forms (monologue, dialogue, polylogue) and the classical «quartet» of illocutionary acts (declarations, directives, commissives). In terms of this harmonious unity, discursive acts (offeratives, con-formatives, accusatives, apologetives, didactives) are developed. The most frequent are offeratives.

Within these speech acts, the Machine implements the offer of services provided to Human. Among the discursive acts that make up the text space of ElDD, prohibitives are not frequent ones because their use is associated with the categorical nature of the Machine, with its frequent «inability» to meet the needs of human.

The act-speech pattern of communication between Human and Machine at the macro level of ElDD is created in at least three ways. First, it is a strategy of effective communication (return, clarification of the request, paraphrasing, simplification), and secondly, it is following the maxims of cooperation (quantity, quality, relevance, method), and thirdly, compliance with the principles of courtesy (tact, approval, modesty, consent). These maxims establish effective communication. Humans rely on their own cognitive-sensory experience and the machine relies on prescribed algorithms, contexts, and templates. In this communication, there are at least two contours, both internal and external. The first is the contextual predetermination of communication, the second is the contour of attraction, which is reflected by the Machine in acts of friendship, sociability, and ethics. In recent years, a special code of ethics for the Machine has been developed, which internalizes impartiality, correctness, reliability of the information, and respect for Human. It also covers issues of privacy and humanity (objectivity of information, adherence to political correctness, avoidance of gender, racial, age discrimination, etc.). Following the principles of Ethics of the Machine, there are certain issues covered:

> Avoid stereotypes *What's your gender?*
> Interpersonal relationships *I am a human too.*
> Personalization *I am a Human. I am not a robot.*
> Peacemaking *Keep calm! Relax. Everything will be fine*
> Humor and friendly communication *Do horses go to Harvard? Horses go to Hayvard*
> (Cleverbot, 2021, EP).

Multimodal interaction of Human and Machine contributes to the gradual formation of a digitalized global world, where the boundaries between Man and Machine are blurred. Animated agents are no longer some images on a computer monitor, but are the embodiment of some anthropomorphic entity, a virtual but equal interlocutor of Human. Going from a mechanical informant and/or automated assistant to a full-fledged interlocutor, the chatbot is gradually transforming into a socially active and sound individual.

Conclusion

The proposed cognitive-communicative analysis of English-language digital discourse may in the future become the basis of linguo-synergetic, linguo-conceptual, linguo-cultural, and linguistic-stylistic descriptions of other digital discourses on the material of different natural languages. The implemented analysis would be helpful for analysis of other discursive formations, conceptual pictures of the world, cognitive and functional comprehension of text spaces, and contrastive research reflections, including translation studies. The phenomenon of ElDD can and should become a source of in-depth cognitive reflections in different fields of humanities, such as psychology, philosophy, cultural studies, and computer science. The introduced approach can also contribute to the expansion of knowledge and ideas of the linguistic community about the role and place of ElDD in neuro-linguistic programming and language manipulation techniques.

References

1. BytePython. URL: https://pythobyte.com/python-keywords-identifiers-7cd08b65/ (accessed: 27.01.2021).

2. Cleverbot. URL: https://www.cleverbot.com/j2convbydate-qg14955 (accessed: 15.05.2021).

3. Farhadi S., Asl H. D., Talebi Z. Morphological Awareness. Iran, 2015. Vol. 5, issue 4. 224 p. URL: https://mjltm.org/article-1-58-en.pdf (accessed: 17.05.2021).

4. Gabbrielli M., Martini S. Programming Languages: Principles and Paradigms, Undergraduate Topics in Computer Science. 2010. URL: http://websrv. dthu.edu.vn/attachments/newsevents/content2415/Programming_Languages_-_Principles_and_Paradigms_thereds1106.pdf (accessed: 27.07.2021).

5. Gee J. P. Unified discourse analysis: Language, reality, virtual worlds, and video games. New York: Routledge. 2014. P. 134–147.

6. Herring S. Computer-mediated discourse analysis: an approach to researching online communities. Designing for Virtual Communities in the Service of Learning. 2004. P. 316–338.

7. Jokuza E. Beyond dimensions: The man who married a hologram. CNN Digital Expansion. 2017. URL: https://edition.cnn.com/2018/12/28/health/rise-of-digisexuals-intl/index.html (accessed: 10.09.2019).

8. Lazebna N. English Language as Mediator of Human-Machine Communication. Mysore, India : PhDians along with Ambishpere; Academic and Medical Publishers ; Royal Book Publishing, 2021. 571 p.

9. Lazebna N., Prykhodko A. Digital discourse of English languageacquisition. Journal of Language and Linguistic Studies, 2021. URL: https://www.jlls.org/index.php/jlls/article/view/2533/852 (accessed: 25.01.2021).

10. Makhachashvili R., Semenist I., Zatsnyi Y., Klymenko O. Digital Interoperability of Foreign Languages Education. DHW 2021: Digital Humanities Workshop, 2021. P. 148–155.

11. Petukhova V., Gropp M., Schmidt A. The DBOX Corpus Collection of Spoken Human-Human and Human-Machine Dialogues. 2014. URL: https://www.researchgate.net/profile/Volha_Petukhova/publication/304625403_The_DBOX_Corpus_Collection_of_Spoken_Human-Human_and_Human-Machine_Dialogues/links/577523ce08ae4645d60ba568/The-DBOX-Corpus-Collection-of-Spoken-Human-Human-and-Human-Machine-Dialogues.pdf (accessed: 25.07.2020).

12.   RecipeQA. 2019. URL: https://hucvl.github.io/recipeqa/ (accessed: 18.12.2019).

13.   Scratch. URL: https://scratch.org/career-guides (accessed: 16.07.2021).

14.   Squeak by Example 5.3. Black A., Ducasse S., Nierstrasz O., Pollet D. USA. 2020. 320 p.

15.   Squeak. URL: https://squeak.com (accessed: 02.02.2021).

16.   VanLeeuwenT. Multimodality. In The Routledge handbook of applied linguistics. Routledge, 2011. P. 688–702.

17.   Yan Z., Duan N., Bao J.-W. DocChat: An information retrieval approach for chatbot engines using unstructured documents. 2016. URL: https://doi.org/10.3390/app10093335 (accessed: 26.07.2021).

Authors' bio

Nataliia Lazebna, Privat Dozent, Dr. Habil. TEFL Metodology Department, New Philological Institute, Julius-Maximilians University of Wuerzburg, Germany, was born on May 15, 1985 in Zaporizhzhia, Ukraine. She defended her Habilitation Project at Zaporizhzhia National University, Zaporizhzhia, Ukraine, in 2021, in the Field of Germanic languages. She obtained degree of Habilitated Doctor of Philological Sciences in the field of Germanic Languages (Confirmed by Zentralstelle für ausländisches Bildungswesen, Bonn, 21/04/2022, with the following Berufliche Anerkennung: habilitierter Wissenschaftler). She obtained her Ph.D. in Philological Sciences in the field of Germanic Languages in 2013 at Donetsk National University, Ukraine. Participated in AE E-Teacher Programs. TESOL Methodology certified (March, 2019). Alumni Cascade OPEN Courses with Colleagues (August - November, 2020). AE E-Teacher TESOL Methodology MOOC Facilitator at University of Maryland Baltimore County (February, 2020). For 15 years she has been working as Associate Professor at Department of Theory and Practice of Translation, Zaporizhzhia National Polytechnic University. The author of more than 50 academic journal articles, conference proceedings, and students' guidelines. The Official Opponent at 8 thesis defenses. The reviewer of vocabularies, monographs, and other printed scientific materials. An experienced translator and academic writer in the American and UK Companies.

Anatoliy Prykhodko, Doctor Habil. in Philology, Full Professor and Chair of Translation Theory and Practice Department at Zaporizhzhia National Polytechnic University, was born in Zaporizhzhia region, Ukraine, on 23 September, 1954. He graduated from Dniepropetrovsk State University in 1976. He got his Ph.D. degree in Philology, Germanic languages, in Kyiv State Pedagogical University of Foreign languages in 1982. He defended his postdoc thesis in 2002, Kyiv Shevchenko National University.
     Starting from 1976, he occupied various positions in Dniepropetrovsk, Kyiv and Zaporizhzhia. He has been delivering lectures in linguistics in Dniepropetrovsk, Kyiv, and Zaporizhzhia and passed his professional training at the universities of Germany (Essen, Han-

nover, Lepzig), including DAAD, Goethe Institute. He now is the Chair of Translation Theory and Practice Department at Zaporizhzhia National Polytechnic University.

Sphere of interest: syntax of Germanic languages, structural linguistic studies, cognitive linguistics, conceptology, linguosynergy, discoursive studies.

Dr. Habil. Prykhodko is a Member of All-Ukrainian Associations of Germanists.

N. Lazebna / D. Kumar (Ed.), Studies in Modern English, Würzburg, 2022, p. 53-61. DOI: 10.25972/WUP-978-3-95826-199-0-53

English Language Variation: Creation of Zambian English (ZamEnglish)

Jive Lubbungu,[*] Ireen Moonga[†], Audrey Muyuni,[‡] Samson Zimba[§]

Abstract

In the present chapter, an attempt has been made to discuss the need to create Zambian English to address English language variations in Zambia. No language in the world can remain the same after interacting with other languages. The present chapter intends to propose and support the idea of using 'Zambian English' for both formal and informal business. Such a measure would create the communicative competence that the majority of the Zambians have always longed for. In Zambia, the purpose of using English language office is to deliberate day to day's business. On the contrary, this has been found to be an obstacle to those who lack principles of command in the language usage, but are able to construct sentences for communicative purposes yet are deprived in international interactions. The views expressed in this chapter are those of the language experts who were engaged in a conversation with regard to the possibility of creating what would be known as Zambian English (ZamEnglish).

Keywords: Zambian English, language variation, speech community.

Background

When we talk of English, we are normally referring to the language of England; the English language variety we refer to in recipient countries as received pronunciation (RP) variety of the English language. This is the kind of English as used by the British Broadcasting Corporation (BBC) in England. Historically, Britain colonised a lot of nations and so wherever people were colonised by Britain, the English language was learnt and used for communication purposes in writing and speech, in both formal and informal circles of life. It was also used in education both as a subject and as a medium of instruction at all levels of education; Primary, Secondary and University. The colonial Government from Britain made it a point that the English language had a policy that assisted in spreading of this selected language; starting in Ireland in the late 12th century and continuing well into the 19th century in Northern Rhodesia (now Zambia). Geographically, the English language is currently spoken

---

[*]   Lecturer, Kwame Nkrumah University, School of Humanities and Social Science, Zambia.
[†]   Lecturer, Mulungushi University, Zambia.
[‡]   Lecturer, Mulungushi University, Zambia.
[§]   Lecturer, Mulungushi University, Zambia.

in all the five continents due to the British policy which allowed it to be deliberately engineered in all British colonies. This originates from a strong saying that says 'The sun never sets in the British Empire' (Bald et al, 2013).

English, thus, is widely used in many varieties throughout the world in its spoken and written forms. For this reason, it is considered to be a global language that has gained currency internationally. English is treated as a means of communication in the areas of the economy, technology, science, arts, tourism, and sports. In their study of English as an Economic language, Zhao and Zhao (2019) established that the relationship of language learning and language application is just like investment and benefit. People use language to transact business and even make a living globally.

The English language functions as an "international" or "world language," and it serves as 'lingua-franca' for facilitating communication between people who do not share the same first (or even second) language (Harmer, 2007). Being a world language, English has been influenced by the many languages that have come in contact with it. The influence from the different languages is normally very prominent phonologically, semantically and even orthographically. Since English is considered to be the most important tool for communication globally, the understanding of its varieties that includes accent also becomes necessary. Aeni, et al (2021:1) explains,

> Accent has different fields: phrase, sentence and sentence.
> The term accent is part of the characteristic way that
> a language is pronounced (also called word stress or
> lexical stress). Different accents have characterised
> the varieties of English spoken in the various areas of the
> world.

This chapter intends to propose and support the idea of using 'Zambian English' for both formal and informal business. Such a measure would create the communicative competence that the majority of the Zambians have always longed for.

English Language Variation in Zambia
Language Variations in Zambia

Zambia is a landlocked country with a total of about seventy-two recognised languages and dialects segmented in different regions. Apart from numerous languages and dialects that have been identified in Zambia, there are seven official vernacular languages: Bemba, Nyanja, Lozi, Tonga, Luvale, Lunda, and Kaonde, the latter three being languages of North-Western Province. In the 19th century the British government colonized central Africa including Zambia and English became the official language of government and is used for education, commerce and law. English became a second language prior to indigenous languages spoken in Zambia. Therefore, principles of English language were taught and learnt officially suppressing the familiar languages which remained as local communicative languages in their original regions. With these remarks it is therefore, important to define what language is and its purpose to human life (encyclopedia Britannica).

What is Language?

The word language has been defined by many scholars, Moeller and Catalano (2015) defined the term language as "the vehicle required for effective human-to-human interactions and yields a better understanding of one's own language and culture." According to Hakim, (2018) Language is a system of conventional, spoken, or written symbols utilized when human beings are communicating. Further, Chomsky (2018) said "the language is the inherent capability of native speakers to understand and form grammatical sentences." Chomsky (2018) also pointed out that a language is a set of (finite or infinite) sentences; each finite length constructed out of a limited set of elements. Hence this definition of language considers sentences as the basis of a language. Sentences may be limited or unlimited and are made up of only minor components.

Additionally, Hakim (2018) showed different definitions included the following; Derbyshire's who said "the language is undoubtedly a kind of communication among human beings. It consists primarily of vocal sounds, articulatory, systematic, symbolic, and are arbitrary."

This definition of Derbyshire clearly indicates that language is the best source of communication, and it also portrays how human language and the fundamental principles of language are formed. According to Lyons, languages are the principal communication systems used by particular groups of human beings within the specific society of which they are members (Hakim, 2018). Lyons specifically points out that language is the best communicative system of human beings by particular social groups. From the few definitions of language given above, it is worth noting that language exists for communicative purpose.

All the above definitions point to the fact that among human beings language is a system of conventional arbitrary symbols, written and spoken in both words and sentences, which are used for communication. The central purpose for having language is for it to facilitate communication among people. The other point to note is that language must be accepted among its users as it must be continually and consistently used the same way among the people that use it.

Language Variations

Cummins (2017) asserted that linguistic variation is central to the study of language use. In fact, it is impossible to study the language forms used in natural texts without being confronted with the issue of linguistic variability. Cummins (2017) postulated that "Variability is inherent in human language: a single speaker will use different linguistic forms on different occasions, and different speakers of a language will express the same meanings using different forms."

He, further, explains that most of this variation is highly systematic. Therefore, speakers of a language make choices in pronunciation, morphology, word choice, and grammar depending on a number of non-linguistic factors. According to Cummins, (2017) "…these factors include the speaker's purpose in communication, the relationship between speaker and hearer, the production circumstances, and various demographic affiliations that a speaker can have." In Zambian context language, variations is experienced more in local languages. One language may be spoken slightly differently and yet maintaining mutual intelligibility. Such variations are referred to dialects. The pronunciations in syllables differ from one language to another.

In Chewa, for instance, the word that means 'with nothing' is cabe (Katete dialect) but Caje (Lundazi Mwase Mphangwe dialect).Because of this, some language groups fail to interpret words from certain varieties of the same language. Similarly, some tribes in Zambia fail to grasp the English syllables and cannot give original meaning and pronunciations of certain words. This is particularly the case where a certain variety of English is used rather than the one people already are used to. English, being the second language, some Zambian tribes find it difficult to bring out the originality of the language.

As a matter of fact, certain pronunciations which are difficult to make are Zambianised, including certain words too. This makes English native speakers, including other non-Zambians who speak English, also find it difficult to fully understand some Zambians. The changes that occur to English cause Zambia to drift away from the English variety as spoken by RP native speakers to what we may call 'Zambian English' which had certain additions or subtractions to both English words and sentences phonologically, morphologically as well as syntactically. The causes are these changes that are happening to the English language of the Received Pronunciation. The English variety of English should be promoted alongside the RP currently used in Zambia. It manages to make people communicate, except it is not allowed officially. Hence, this chapter advocates for less measures to be taken in usage of rule-governed English for communicative purposes locally and internationally (Bloomfield, 1914).

English as an official Language in Zambia

Studying a language provides the learner with an opportunity to gain linguistic and social knowledge, and to know when, how, and why to say what to whom (National Standards in Foreign Language Education Project-NSFLEP, 2014). English language, like any other language or skill, is learnt through language learning and acquisition. Language scholars distinguish between the terms acquisition and learning. Canale and Swain (2019) refer to 'acquisition' as the process of learning first and second languages naturally, without formal instruction, whereas 'learning' is reserved for the formal study of second or foreign languages in classroom settings.

In Zambia, foreign language education is mostly done in schools through formal instruction. It mostly follows the learning approach or deliberate instruction. However, like any other language, it can also be learnt informally through acquisition.

Whether English is learnt formally or informally, there is a chance that this foreign language can drift away from RP to a Zambian variety (Zambian English) through pronunciation and borrowing which includes localization of both phonological and morphological aspects of the foreign or second languages to the indigenous ones. Currently, the Zambian English variety is not recognised in public as well as education circles. To state it clearly, the Zambian English variety is not allowed everywhere in Zambia. This is the case because the current language policy on the learning and use of English is that all Zambians should learn the British Received Pronunciation (RP) kind of English.

This chapter intends to state that the role of language is to facilitate communication, the role the Zambian variety of English plays among the Zambian users. This study is advocating for the promotion and legalisation of Zambian English alongside RP for effective communication among both the educated and the not-so-educated. What is required is to deliberately promote it. It is believed the political will, through the language policy can make this dream come true.

Foreign language education does not refer to the teaching of a modern language that is neither an official language nor the mother tongue of a significant part of the population. In case of Zambia, English and the seven distinguished indigenous languages are taught and examined at national level and are used professionally. Whereas French, Portuguese and Chinese are considered foreign languages, English is a second and official language in Zambia.

English as Foreign Language in Zambia

According to Moeller and Catalano (2015) foreign language learning and teaching refer to the teaching or learning of a non-native language outside of the environment where it is commonly spoken. A language is considered foreign if it is learned largely in the classroom, and is not spoken in the society where the teaching occurs. In the Zambian context, the English language is taught in school and pupils hardly speak it correctly, Therefore, it seems to be a continuous learning process. As such, English is relevant for communication purposes in terms of school, commerce and law. Chapelle (2010) observed that "learning another language provides access into a perspective other than one's own, increases the ability to see connections across content areas, and promotes an interdisciplinary perspective while gaining intercultural understandings." Therefore, study of another language allows the individual to communicate effectively and creatively and to participate in real life situations through the language of the authentic culture itself.

In Zambia, the purpose of using English language officially is to deliberate the day-to-day's business. On the contrary, this has been found to be an obstacle to those who lack principles of command in the language usage but are able to construct sentences for communicative purposes. At the same time, they are also deprive of international interactions.

Error Analysis

A number of studies have been carried out on the analysis of errors especially in the English Language. Scholars like Moonga (2012) defined an error, quoting Brown (1980: 166) as "…a process carried out to observe, analyse and classify the deviations of the second language…in order to reveal the systems operated by the learners."

Most of the errors are in form of spelling, morphology, syntax (grammar), punctuation, lexical and semantic choice, style and typography. However, in terms of the Zambian situation, and indeed, many other countries, mother toungue (L1) influence cannot be overlooked as it characterises second language learners' speech and orthography. Since L1 is well known by most users, it could be a stepping stone to the needed proficiency in the second language acquisition.

Zambian English: Experts' Opinions in Zambia

A number of language experts were engaged in a conversation via a WhatsApp platform on the need to create what would be called Zambian English. Different views and opinions were brought forward in an attempt to consider coming up with Zambian English. Some participants made reference to how America devised their own English which is known as American English. In the Zambian situation, examples such as "sheet bed" for "bed sheet", "switch off the lights" for "turn off the lights", "last of last week, next of next week" for "last week, but one, next week but one or after next week," and the statement "I went to a restaurant and I had to buy drinks" instead of "I went to a restaurant and bought drinks" would constitute Zambian English. The argument brought forward was that although the English is wrongly followed the conventional way of sentence construction, what matters is to communicate. One of the participants remarked thus:

> If you look at the American vs English words, it is the same word or term spelt and said differently. Can we try that, e.g. "bed sheet vs sheet bed" as a good example of Zambianising English.

For example, the expression 'Yotam is movious' to mean either 'Yotam likes wandering' or 'Yotam does not like staying at home' is understood by Zambians. It just needs to be popularized in the world to be accepted as part of the English language. Secondly, all translated nouns, like Yohan from John, Yosefe from Joseph could be used as they occur in Zambian languages. In this case, we are referring to a modern language that is neither an official language nor the mother tongue, but caters for a significant part of the Zambian population.

Further, justification for the formation of Zambian English (ZamEnglish) was based on how the Americans simplified English Orthography and phonetics. A word should be pronounced the way it is written. For example, where do the British see the 'f' in lieutenant? That is why, American pronounce it as [lutenanti] instead of British [lefutenanti]. Although some participants questioned this view as they considered it as a result of the influence of the French, since English borrowed most of the words from French and to some extent Latin, the call to focus on Zam English was louder. One participant argued that:

> I feel Zambian English can be constituted by our social cultural context directly translated to English like Nigerian. For example, I know of one village old man who uses 'cry' in the place of 'mourning' and 'drink medicine' instead of 'take medicine'. Correctness of language is determined by acceptability by the speech community. In Nigeria for instance, most speech domains have done away with 'lend' as they use 'borrow' for both giving and getting. The subject and object determines whether one is giving or getting.

Moonga (2012) used the following social cultural as well as translation errors that she analysed during her study:

1. Please teacher, may I be allowed to go home and enter someone's clay pot (Literal Tonga translation for undergoing steaming-treatment due to sickness)
2. When I was in Grade 10, I was suffering a phone so that I could be communicating with other people (Meaning: I needed a phone for communication with other people)

The sentences above are literal translations that are meeting the criteria for communicative competence within the cultural and social contexts. If such Zam English was formalised, communication would be made easy across social cultural groupings.

Furthermore, based on the above argument, there should be no need to worry about the correctness of English, and therefore, broken English would qualify as Zambian English. It is only broken when you compare it with British or American. One participant submitted that:

> There should be a level of self-esteem in us. That makes those we call powerful in most of the things. If others will see it as local or broken English but accept it and use it as Zambian, then let us start it. It is okay and Zambian English could be a reference too. Why not?

Another participant added that Zambian English words can be coined based on the pronunciation such as 'ch' of British to be written as 'c.' Hence, 'chocolate' becomes 'cokolete', 'church' becomes 'cece' while 'shoes' becomes 'shuzi'. Further, words like 'geo' becomes 'jo' and get 'jofuri' instead of 'Geoffrey.' Such an approach would make it easy for Zambians to pronounce words and communicate without difficulty.

However, some views were contrary to the idea of creating ZamEnglish as the approach was perceived to be neo-colonialistic, and therefore, there was the need to innovate. This can only be done by adopting an African or Zambian language that can be used for communication. In Zambia, a lingua-franca 'Nyanja' can be adopted just as Tanzania has adopted Swahili in their communication. Zambia can then aspire to improve Nyanja so that it is not misconstrued as a regional language since it is not derived from any particular tribe in Zambia.

Proposed Future Research

It would be good to undertake research regarding ZamEnglish among all the different ethnic groups in Zambia so that the results would be generalised to the whole country, thus, promoting unity. Participants would be sourced among English and Zambian Language academicians from Secondary schools, colleges and Universities. Another study on how teachers can engage learners in identifying ways of how L1 can be used to enhance proficiency and competence in L2 could be carried out.

Conclusion

ZamEnglish would improve the interaction and cooperation levels between the educated and those that may not have had a chance of attaining formal education in Zambia. It is a well known fact in Zambia that, though not openly pronounced, there are social classes between the elite that speak standard English, (RP) and those that use English communicatively. ZamEnglish would bridge this gap. Furthermore, ZamEnglish, could be a uniting factor among the various ethnic groups in the multilingual society of Zambia. As a result, all the workers would be motivated to develop a sense of belongingness, national identity and ownership since they would already hold a shared vision through the common language. With the dawn of globalisation, ZamEnglish may just be a stepping stone to attain unity in diversity through the liberal minds that are more likely to embrace change for sustainable communication skills.

References

1.   Aeni, N. M. Octaberlina, L. R., Lubis, N. D. A. (2021). A Literature Review of English Variation on Sociolinguistics. doi: 10.31219/osf.io/ehx2q

2.   Bald, V., Chatteji, M., Reddy S., & Vimalassery, M. (2013). The Sun Never Sets. New York. New York University Press.

3.   Bloomfield, L. (1914). *An introduction to the study of language.* New York: Henry Holt and Company.

4.   Brown, D. H. (1980). Principles of Learning and Teaching. New Jersey: Prentice Hall.

5.   Canale, M., Swain, M. (2019). Theoretical bases of communicative approaches to second language teaching and testing. *Journal of Applied Linguistics* 1, pp. 1–47.

6.   Chapelle, C. (2010). *If Intercultural Competence is the Goal, What are the Materials?* In: Proceedings of CERCLL Intercultural Competence Conference. CERCLL, Tucson, Arizona, pp. 27–50.

7.   Chomsky, N. (1959). *Review of verbal behavior by B.F. Skinner.* Language 35, pp. 26–58.

8.   Cummins, J. (2017). Rethinking monolingual instructional strategies in multilingual classrooms. *Canadian Journal of Applied Linguistics* (CJAL) 10, pp. 221–241.

9.   Encyclopedia Britannica Inc. People of Zambia: Ethnic and Linguistic Composition pp. 322-350

10.   Hakim, A. (2018). *Definitions of Language by Different Scholars and Linguists.* New York; English Finders.

11.   Moeller, A. K and Catalano, T. (2015) Foreign Language Teaching and Learning. *International Encyclopedia of the Social & Behavioral Sciences,* 2nd ed. pp. 327–33.

12.   Moonga, I. (2012). An analysis of written errors commited by Grade 11 pupils in a multilingual context: A case of selected schools in Kabwe and Monze Districts of Zambia. MA Dissertation-UNZA.

13.   National Standards in Foreign Language Education Project (NSFLEP), 2014. World Readiness Standards for Learning Languages (WRSLL). Alexandria. VA. Online https://www.actfl.org/resources/world-readiness-standards-learning-languages

14.   Zhao, C. and Zhao, Y. (2019) Study on Business English Practical Teaching from the Perspective of Economics of Language. *Creative Education*, 10, pp. 726-734. doi: 10.4236/ce.2019.104054.

Authors' bio

Ireen Moonga has been working as a lecturer and researcher at Mulungushi university, Zambia. Her research areas comprise language development and implementation. She has participated in number of international conferences. Besides, she got a number of research articles published in reputed journals.

Audrey Muyuni Phiri is working as a lecturer at Public University, Zambia. Regarding Publication, her areas of interest include Internationalism of Higher Education and Value of doctoral education.

Zimbu Samson has been working as a lecturer at Mulungushi University. His areas of interest include Linguistic, especially focusing on syntax, phonetic, morphology, semantic and pragmatism.

Jive Lubbungu is currently working as a lecturer at Kevin University School of humanity and social sciences in department of literature and language issues.

N. Lazebna / D. Kumar (Ed.), Studies in Modern English, Würzburg, 2022, p. 63-72. DOI: 10.25972/WUP-978-3-95826-199-0-63

The Relationship between Language, Culture, and Development of Society

Kateryna Lut,[*] Hanna Starenkova[†]

Abstract

The paper analyses specific characteristics of language that influence the development of culture and societies. The problem of the connection between language and culture has occupied the minds of many famous scientists: some believe that language is a part of the culture as a whole; others think that language is only a form of cultural expression. Undoubtedly, language constitutes a vital component of the cultural background underlying social development. Language is an essential means of communication and interaction. However, language is at the same time sovereign about culture as a whole and can be separate from culture or compared to culture as an equal element (i.e., that language is neither a form nor a component of culture).

Keywords: language, culture, expression, development, communication, interaction, component, social, connection, background

Introduction

Communication is an essential element of any society, and language is a key aspect of that. Different cultural communities put together collective understandings through sounds as language began to develop. Eventually, these sounds and their implicit meanings became ordinary and language was formed. A symbolic process whereby social reality is constructed, maintained, repaired, and transformed is called intercultural communication. The language barrier is one of the most difficult moments in the interaction of people with different cultural backgrounds. Ethnicity, gender, geographic location, religion, language, and so much more are those factors on which cultural identity is heavily dependent. Culture is determined as an originally transmitted structure of symbols, meanings, and norms (Geertz, 1993). An important part of cultural exchange is the connection – in the case when knowing a language automatically enables someone to identify with others who speak the same language. Learning a language can be daunting, but it is an important way to communicate with people from different cultures.

---

[*]   Assistant Professor, Candidate of Philological Sciences, Zaporizhzhia Polytechnic National University, Zaporizhzhia, Ukraine.

[†]   Master's Student in Philology, Zaporizhzhia Polytechnic National University, Zaporizhzhia, Ukraine.

This article addresses the problems of the interaction between language, culture, and societal development and offers certain conclusions concerning specific language characteristics connected with such an interaction. **The purpose** of the article is to determine the specificities of the interaction between culture and language and their influence on the development of society. The purpose involves solving the following tasks:

- consider the features of language that relate to cultural and social aspects;
- determine the ways culture and language interact;
- identify the ways language and culture influence the development of societies.

Literature review

The indisputable and obvious connection between language and culture as a serious scientific problem was posed at the beginning of the nineteenth century in the works of W. von Humboldt (Humboldt, 1999). This connection was studied within the framework of such disciplines as ethnolinguistics, anthropology, linguistic pragmatics, and sociolinguistics. V.V. Vorobyov considered the relationship between culture and language within the science of linguoculturology. He explained that the main object of linguoculturology becomes "interrelation and interaction of culture and language in the process of its functioning and study of interpretation this interaction in a single system integrity" (Vorobyov, 1997, p. 36-37). The hypothesis of E. Sapir - B. L. Whorf (Sapir, 1961; Whorf, 1956) became a prerequisite for the emergence of linguoculturology. They put forward a deep hypothesis of linguistic relativity, according to which language is assigned a priority role in the process of cognition. Thanks to this hypothesis, a new direction of linguistics has been formed – ethnolinguistics with linguoculturology arising it, which studies the relationship of people, ethnic groups, and language in the field of culture. Professor Z.K.Tarlanov defines the inextricable link between the language and the ethnos. Thus, language is a form of culture that embodies the historically developing national type of life in all its diversity and dialectical inconsistency (Tarlanov, 1993). The issue of language and cultural interaction has always been controversial and occupied the minds of other famous scientists and researchers (J. L. Austin, Erasov B. S., L. Bollinger, E. Sapir, P. Trudgill, and so on) (Austin, 1975; Erasov, 2003; Bollinger, 1993; Sapir, 1961; Trudgill, 1995).

Methodology

The material of this article is the development and analysis of the literature of well-known researchers. Also, the article is built on the basis of our research and this synthesis has become a great foundation in this matter. Thus, the results and conclusions of the research scientists have become the basis for this article.

Results

For centuries, the issue of the relationship between language and culture has occupied the minds of many famous scientists, but to this day the problem remains disputable: some believe that language is a part of the culture as a whole, while others think that language is only a form of cultural expression.

Communication can be realized in three different ways: via spoken words, written words, or drawings and paintings. However, an individual can also use other ways to create and convey symbols. For example, a person symbolizes with the help of personal gestures like hugs, handshakes, winks, or nods. Bells, beacons, carrier pigeons, tattoos, and tantalizing perfumes are also used by humans to convey meanings. In short, man's modes of communication include all the procedures by which one member of the communication act may influence another. However, such ways of communication are uniquely associated with human beings, and the ability to learn and use the language is the most significant distinction between human and animal societies.

Society and culture affect the words that we use for a speech act, and the words for this act of communication, in their turn, influence society and culture. Such a cyclical interdependence might seem complicated, but many examples from our lives support and demonstrate this connection. One of the best ways to learn about these three components: society, culture, and language, is to seek out new possibilities to investigate this issue. Language not only reflects and reveals highlights and observations; it also has an impact on attitudes and behaviour.

Every social organization requires some means (Internet, live communication, discussions, debates, verbal and non-verbal acts, as well as other ways of connection) through which communicators can interchange their ideas, share information, convey a set of meanings, and achieve some degree of mutual understanding. They also allow people to come to a consensus. It is only when this consensus exists that people can interconnect, i.e., in this case, they can make fairly exact predictions about each other's behaviour. In other words, such a social interaction among human groups may be impossible without significant means of communication. This interaction is largely carried out through the use of signs in both human and animal societies.

Natural and Conventional. Whereas sub-humans use widely natural signs, human groups on the other hand communicate with each other through conventional signs or symbols. Sub-humans are therefore said to apply both language and symbols since they cannot abstract a concept from a particular concrete context. That is why language is restricted to human beings.

Bollinger characterized language as a system of vocal-auditory communication using conventional signs constructed of arbitrary patterned sound units and assembled according to set when interacting with the experiences of its members (Bollinger, 1993). George Mead (Mead, 1934) considered that language is possible wherever a stimulus can affect the other. It is explained in this way: when essential symbols arouse in an individual the same reactions as they explicitly cause or are supposed to call in other individuals to whom they are addressed. Language is said to come into being when two or more humans have learnt to fasten the same values or experiences to the same sound combinations. Technically, language is not restricted to purely verb expressions but involves any standardized and conventionalized system of symbols. Therefore, language is not only a system of words or symbols. Most likely, it is a form of behaviour involving the use and interpretation of symbols.

With respect to the definitions above, a logical question arises: what functions does language have for society? R. Jakobson (Jakobson, 1956) identifies the following functions:

- The referential function: refers to the part of the context and describes a situation, mental state or object. The descriptive components of the referential function can include both explicit descriptions and deictic words. Similarly, the referential function is connected with an element whose true meaning is under questioning especially when the true meaning is identical in both the real and assumptive universe.
- The poetic function: concentrates on "the message for its own sake" (how the code is employed) and is the efficient function in poetry as well as slogans.
- The emotive function: refers to the sender and is best illustrated by interjections and other sound changes that do not change the denotative meaning of a statement but do add information about the speaker's internal state. Whether a person has feelings of happiness, sadness, grief or otherwise, this function is used to express different emotions.
- The conative function: engages the receiver directly and is best described by vocatives and imperatives.
- The phatic function: is a language for the sake of interplay and is therefore connected with the contact/channel factor. The phatic function can be observed in greetings and casual discussions, especially with strangers. It also provides the means to open, maintain, verify or close the communication channel.
- The metalingual/reflexive function: is the use of language (what is called code) to discuss or describe itself.

The connection between culture and language can be traced in such functions of the language as referential, emotive, and metalingual. The former is related to the fact that it describes the situation, behavior, and mental state when a person uses language. Thus, language and culture influence the formation of thinking, perception of the world, and behavior. The emotive function focuses on the speaker, their emotions and attitudes. Consequently, it is connected with expressing all that is specific for the culture, behavioral patterns, mentality, etc., of an ethnic group. The last function directly concerns the way we use the language. That is, a person uses different spheres of vocabulary, and language tools, depending on the situation, culture here plays the role of an auxiliary element for the language and its use.

In this way, human culture and language are deeply tied. Without becoming familiar with a language, anthropologists would have some difficulties understanding a culture. Consequently, language cannot exist without culture and vice versa.

Communication between humans is meaningful and this is its specific feature. The language applies arbitrary signs to explain some ideas and facts to transfer meaning. People communicate over and over again with each other: in spoken, written forms, or via gestures. As a result, language's main value and meaning go beyond its signs or symbols. With the help of language, humans can share beliefs, worries, perceptions, expectations, experiences, and knowledge. These are so-called building blocks of spoken culture.

According to the Sapir-Whorf hypothesis (linguistic relativity (Sapir, 1961; Whorf, 1956)), it is suggested that a language and its overarching components or structures used for classifying the world directly shape man's perceptions. Therefore, speakers of distinct languages are likely to perceive the world differently. Another important finding was that cultural relativity is the key to understanding the impact of culture on human interactions. If a head wants to create and manage global teams that can interact together successfully, he/she needs to understand not just how people from his/her cultural experience people from different international cultures, but also how those international cultures perceive one another.

It is possible to hypothesize that these conditions are likely to occur in the importance of sociolinguistics. In general, sociolinguistics is the study of language that relates to social structure and additional components (gender, age, religion, geography, social class and status, education, occupation, ethnicity, nationality, and identity) (Trudgill, 1995). This definition allows to suggest that language is constantly changing. Accordingly, social norms and practices influence the ways that people speak with each other. Thus, we can deduce certain conclusions about relationships and relative status in society of human groups by looking at how people speak to each other.

In some cases, due to gender or age people are restricted from speaking in certain situations. These findings prove that sociolinguists pay attention to this controversial nature of language, including how more than one exclusive variant of a language can exist among its users.

These results are likely to be related to diglossia. This term is used to show the situation in which two languages (or two varieties of the same language) are used under different conditions within a community, often by the same speakers. This phenomenon refers to the existence of two different ways of speaking (or "registers") within a single language, typically with a "high" or formal variety and a "low" or informal, everyday variety. In this way, speakers consciously select which register to use based on accepted social conditions. For instance, one might speak differently when chatting with friends versus when addressing a college professor.

In addition, there is also such a concept as code-switching. In this sense, bilingual, multilingual, and plurilingual people may likewise switch from one language to another in the course of a conversation with one or more participants. The motivations for switching codes in mid-conversation can range from a polite attempt to include nearby speakers of other languages, to a deliberate political act of defiance. This combination of findings allows us to validate the fact that language is one of the most essential parts of any culture. It is the way with the help of which people communicate with one another, build strong relationships, and create a sense of collectivity.

According to Erasov B.S, (Erasov, 2003, p. 23-26) "culture can be defined as what this society does and thinks, and language is what it thinks". The relationship between culture and language can be described as the relationship between the whole and its part. Language can be interpreted as an essential component of culture or an instrument of culture. However, language is at the same time sovereign concerning culture as a whole and can be separate from culture or compared to culture as an equal element (i.e., that language is neither a form nor a component of culture).

Culture can be a sensitive topic. Speaking about a person's culture often provokes the same type of reaction as speaking about his/her mother. Most people have a deep protective instinct in relation to culture they consider their own, and, though they may even criticize it bitterly themselves, they may become easily get angry if someone from outside the culture dares to do so.

When you are in and of culture (comparison can be as fish are in and of water) it is often difficult or even impossible to see that culture. Often people who have spent their lives living in one culture observe only regional and individual differences and therefore assume, "My national culture does not have a clear character".

The understanding of culture is associated with a developing attitude towards language. By the beginning of the 21st century, linguistics has gone through a full cycle of some kind of evolution: from completely disregarding extra-linguistic effects to realizing the need for a detailed analysis of socio-cultural, communicative, psychological, situational, and contextual conditions of language communication act. It should be mentioned that if the 1970s of the 20th century were the "boom of semantics", the 1980s were the bloom of the communicative approach to language, the end of the 20th century. The changes in modern language have come to the fore, they (changes) were caused by the "transformation of socio-cultural paradigms", socio-political movements in different countries, and other external, extra-linguistic factors that often become determinants of language modifications. In this way, new linguistic contexts are forming new cultures in society.

Obviously, every nation has its own history, its culture has been created over centuries, and the main unique feature of every nation is its language. Only language reflects all the specific traits and subtleties of this or that nation. Moreover, language mirrors human thinking. It is logical that every nation has its national language. The notion "culture" most often determines the level of human development and in this case this term is synonymous with the concept "civilization". Also, the word "culture" can mean a degree of human spiritual evolution and the level of education. If it comes to the culture of the people, we can indicate folk customs and traditions, specificities of everyday life, etc. The interconnection between language and culture is a complex and multidimensional issue.

The question of the correlation between language and culture has always been of great interest to researchers in various fields: philosophers, sociologists, linguists, psychologists, linguoculturalists, and others. It is no wonder, that each culture has its own language system, through which its speakers have the possibility to communicate with each other. Thus, the value of language in the culture of any nation can hardly be overestimated.

Language reflects the culture, it represents not only the real world surrounding a human, not only the actual conditions of his/her life but also the public mind of the people, their mentality, national character, traditions, customs, moral norms, the system of values, worldview, vision of the world. It is impossible to consider the language of a nation without taking into account its culture and national characteristics; language and culture cannot be separated. In this way, the language of a nation's culture is formed simultaneously. Eventually, the language changes as well as the culture of the society. New values appear in the culture, new expressions take place in the language; new technologies occur in the society – new words develop in the language.

Culture as a subject of study of cultural anthropology is a set of results of human social activity in all spheres of life and all factors (ideas, beliefs, customs, traditions) that constitute and govern the way of life of a nation, class, group of people in a certain period of time. Cultural anthropology studies the progress of culture in all its components: the way of life, vision of the world, mentality, national character, and results of spiritual, social, and working activities of a person. Cultural anthropology explores the unique human capacity to develop culture through communication, including speech and considers the great diversity of human cultures, their interaction, and conflicts. The interaction of language and culture plays a special role nowadays.

The concept that language forms human thinking, made it possible to put the study of thought on a precise effective (linguistic) basis. The dynamics of linguistic facts and the evolution of grammatical categories is accepted as a form of thought movement.

It is worth paying special attention to the relationship and interaction between language and reality, language and culture. These problems are fundamental both for the development of the forms and efficiency of communication and for teaching foreign languages; their disregard explains many failures in international contacts and teaching practices. The most accepted metaphor in the discussion of this topic: language reflects the world, it represents reality and forms its picture of the world, special and unique for each language and, therefore, for each people, ethnic group, and speech community using the language as a means of communication. The closest interconnection and interdependence between the language and its speakers is evident and beyond any doubt. Everyone knows that language is a means of communication between people, and it is inseparably linked to the life and development of the speech group that employs it as an instrument of communication.

Thus, a human takes place between language and the real world. It is the person who experiences and perceives the world through the senses and on this foundation creates a system of ideas and beliefs about the world. Having passed them through his or her mind, having realized the results of this interpretation, he or she transmits them to other members of his or her speech group with the help of language. In other words, between reality and language thinking appears.

The word does not demonstrate the subject of reality itself, but its vision. It (the word) is imposed on the native speaker by the concept of the subject in his/her mind. The concept is formed at the level of generalization of some basic attributes that compose this concept, and therefore represents an abstraction, distraction from specific characteristics. The transformation from the real world to the concept and further to verbal expression is diverse for different peoples. This is caused by distinctions in history, geography, traits of life of these ethnic groups and, accordingly, by differences in the evolution of their social consciousness. Since our mind is determined both collectively (way of life, customs, traditions, etc., i.e., everything that was defined by the notion "culture" in its broad, ethnographic meaning) and individually (specific interpretation of the world appropriate to this particular individual), the language mirrors a reality not directly but in two paradigms: from the real world to thinking and from thought to language. The metaphor with the mirror is no longer as exact as it seemed at first because the mirror turns out to be crooked: its distortion is due to the culture of the speaking group, its mentality, worldview or vision of the world.

Conclusions

Language, thought, and culture are so closely interconnected that they in fact constitute a single whole, containing these three components, neither of which can function and exist without the other two. Altogether, they relate to the real world, oppose it, depend on it, represent and at the same time shape it.

Language and culture interact closely in different ways. In some situations, they complement each other, as in the case of the language functions described above. These two important elements greatly influence the development of society. Thus, people use registers depending on the situation of communication, and select different layers of vocabulary that are suitable in a particular language environment. Culture affects person's values, traditions, and methods of interplay while language facilitates those interactions. Language allows people to interact, and culture suggests them how to do so correctly. In reality, language is used to convey cultural ideas and beliefs. Moreover, both culture and language permit us to look backward in history.

Societal norms were created to structure the ways people communicate with each other. They concern not only with non-verbal communication but also with the language people use to communicate in different situations. Language shapes our cultural identities and the ways we interact in society. The norms and rules acceptable in our own culture facilitate the interaction but that can lead to misunderstanding when used in other cultural contexts. Consequently, in order to suit different surroundings, we need to adapt to other cultural contexts by learning the language, changing our behavior according to societal requirements, and respecting customs and traditions.

Language, as a way of expressing thought and transmitting it from person to person, is closely connected with thinking. The correlation between language and thought is an eternal complex issue and linguistics and philosophy. Further research should be undertaken to investigate the relationship between culture and language and its strong influence on the development of society more deeply. Despite these promising results, questions remain. As we can see, language and culture are interconnected, and it is obvious that they influence society and its members.

References

1.   Austin, J. (1975). *How to Do Things with Words*. Oxford University Press.

2.   Bollinger, L. (1993). *Language*. Journal of the Linguistic Society of America.

3.   Erasov, B. S. (2003). *Social culturology*, 23-26 p. Aspect Press, Moscow.

4.   Geertz, C. (1993). *The Interpretation of Cultures*. Fontana Press, London.

5.   Jakobson, R. (1956). *Fundamentals of Language*. 96 p. Mouton DeGruyter.

6.   Mead, G.H. (1934). *The Background of the Genesis of the Self*, 144-152 p. University of Chicago.

7.   Sapir, E. (1961). *Culture, Language and Personality*. University of California Press.

8.   Tarlanov, Z.K. (1993). *Language, Ethnos, Time,* 165-170 p. Essays on Russian and General Linguistics, Petrozavodsk.

9.   Trudgill, P. (1995). *Sociolinguistics: An introduction to language and society*. 240 p. Penguin Books, London.

10.   Vorobyov, V.V. (1997). *Linguoculturology: theory and methods,* 331 p. Moscow.

11.   Humboldt W. (1999). *On the Diversity of Human Language Construction and Its Influence on the Mental Development of the Human Species*. 296 p. Cambridge University Press.

12.   Whorf, B.L. (1956). *Language, Thought and Reality*. 302 p. MIT, New York: J.Wilky/ London: Chapinaon & Hall.

Authors' bio

Kateryna Lut was born in Zaporizhzhia, Ukraine, November 13, 1980, attended Zaporizhzhia National University (Zaporizhzhia, Ukraine), majored in Philology and in 2003 got Master's degree (with honors). In 2014 completed candidate's (pre-doctorate) thesis. Doctor of Philosophy (2014), specialization field – Germanic languages. Thesis title – Means of Expressiveness in English Economic Discourse: Cognitive and Pragmatic Aspects. After graduating from university, she started her work at Zaporizhzhia National Technical University, first as a Lecturer of the Department of Foreign Languages (2003 – 2010), then as a Lecturer of the Department of Theory and Practice of Translation (2010 – 2014). From 2014 to present, she is an Associate Professor of the Department of Theory and Practice of Translation in National University "Zaporizhzhia Polytechnic" (Zaporizhzhia, Ukraine). She teaches Practice of Translation from English, Practical Course of French, Contrastive Stylistics, and Methodology for teaching foreign languages and translation.

   She has published dozens of articles, including Expressing Attitude in English and Ukrainian Economic Media Discourse (Wydawnictwo Akademii Polonijnej "Educator", 2020), co-authored Readiness of University Teachers to Participate in Empirical Data Exchange: Pilot Study in Ukraine (Magnanimitas Assn, 2021). She is also a co-author of a grammar book Practical English Grammar: Noun. Adjective. Verb. (National University "Zaporizhzhia Polytechnic", 2019). Her areas of interest include Stylistics, Discourse analysis, Theories and practices of translation, and Teaching methods.

Hanna Starenkova was born in Autonomous Republic of Crimea, Ukraine, January 22, 2000, in 2021 got Bachelor's Degree, majored in Philology and Technical translation. Specialization field – Germanic languages and literature (translation inclusive).

She is currently getting a Master's degree at the NU "Zaporizhzhia Polytechnic". She participated in student conferences, competitions and other activities of the university. One of the topics was *"O. Wilde's world perception and his view on the concept of "aesthetism"".* She also participated in an online conference with the topic *"Actualization of the "WORK" concept in English and French languages".*

N. Lazebna / D. Kumar (Ed.), Studies in Modern English, Würzburg, 2022, p. 73-79. DOI: 10.25972/WUP-978-3-95826-199-0-73

ESL/EFL in Teaching and Learning Process

Gladys G. Mangada[*]

> If a teacher is indeed wise, he does not bid you enter the home of his wisdom, but rather leads you to the threshold of your own mind. - Kahlil Gibran

Abstract

Teaching comprises all types of disciplines and teachers need to look outside the confines of English as a Second Language. The acquisition of knowledge comes in a variety of the learners' educational potential. English as a Second Language in teaching and learning, focuses on active learner's involvement and reduction of coercion. Indeed, Gibran's thoughts remain true that "wisdom leads one to discuss his or her potentials. To realize this, teachers in all educational levels have to portray a less dominant classroom role in accord with the importance of classroom interaction in the teaching learning process.

N.A. Flaunders retorted that "in the average classroom someone is talking for two-thirds of the time, two-thirds of the task is direct influence." What does this mean? Students' participation or interaction in the classroom has a significant content to enhance their linguistic competence and its core basis is how to use the language as the most important factor in the classroom. Comprehending the information caters one to establish a fair and well-balanced condition that teachers are facilitators, and the learners are to stay in the frontline.

In today's classroom setting, the adoption-adaption of teaching strategies focuses on the learners' ability to have a strong command or fluency of the language. ESL is learned around the globe and the learners' interests are the primary goals in the teaching and learning process. Colin Blakemore once said that "True knowledge, as Plato argues, must be within us all, and learning consists of solely of discussing what we already know."

In an ESL classroom, discovery of knowledge is not a new game. Teachers do perform their tasks and the learners serve not as passive listeners but as active recipients in the transformation-sharing of all the five macro skills namely speaking, reading, writing, listening, and viewing. In fact, if commitment, knowledge of subject-matter for independent learning, and management of learning are packaged in one big box, both the teachers and the learners will operate a mutual process of generating a lively culture and quality of educational life.

With the aforementioned views I had experienced in teaching ESL, the teacher's passion for teaching and attitude in dealing with the learners create a strong impact on the learners cognitive, affective, and psychomotor domains.

---

[*] Associate Professor, University of Eastern Philippine, University Town, Catarman Northern Samar.

ESL Teaching in the Classroom: A Closer Look

Learners study in different time zones and the process of learning matters based on the skills acquired in and out of the classroom. Each individual's performance in the learning of English holds the belief that exposure to English may not necessarily mean greater proficiency unless the learner is actively involved in the learning process. A necessary prod to active involvement is motivation.

Motivation (acronym form) in ESL teaching

Medium of instruction is English for non-native speakers who are learning in English. Bernardo (2004) in his paper "Non-Native English Students Learning in English: Reviewing and Reflecting on the Research looked into the experiences of bilingual learners as they undertake learning activities in English which is a second or a foreign language for them. Different insights were drawn from the various studies reviewed were expounded as to how bilingual learners use their multilingual resources to attain their learning goals. One of the recommendations calls to study the experiences of bilingual learners' experiences in learning English and reflections for ESL and EFL teachers and other teachers of bilingual learners.

Olshtain (1990) enumerated factors predictive to success or failure in second language and foreign language learning among different learner groups. These are the (a) *the learner context* or the learning conditions formal and informal learning situations; (b) the *social context* which refers to attitudes and motivation deriving from political, cultural, and sociolinguistic milieu; and (c) the *learner's characteristics* encompassing language aptitude, academic knowledge of one's first language and IQ level, as well as other individual features. Students from less advantaged backgrounds have difficulty acquiring the linguistic competence necessary to cope with their school works and one of the major causes for luck of success in school. These factors hold true among the learners inability to reach out and optimize the usage of the language.

Teachers of ESL therefore should know the ways students learn and the components of critical and creative thinking. Learning is a reflective process whereby the learners develop new insights and understanding or changes and restructures the learners' mental process. Learning combines inductive and deductive thoughts whereas learning connotes a general process, critical thinking and creativity refer to specific aspects of learning. Language educators often come across obstacles caused by the hesitance and inhibitions of the learners towards learning the language. In essence, imparting learners' understanding coupled with the teachers' critical reflection is beneficial to their teaching practice.

Interest in learning English and teaching the course in all levels presents a huge scope of involvement from both parties. Learning from different tasks executed in the classroom matters based on the learners' needs. To borrow the words of Bernardo (2004),"language is used in the task and the language skills of the learner. Proficiency in language use will effectively learn or perform different learning tasks when these tasks involve materials not in their native language particularly English as a second language." In fact, it has become more challenging for both teachers and the learners engaging in ESL since the pandemic occurred. The COVID-19 has enforced a new normal setting and environment for learning, thus the pedagogy has evolved to conform to the current needs in the academe.

Variety of teaching strategies applies to learners' needs as they traverse the path of learning. It does not dwell on the teacher's dominant attitude in the classroom but simply delivers or introduces activities that would enhance students' interests and this can be achieved by encouraging students feel better and express their ideas in English to acquire more English words and expand their knowledge pool. Various categories were taken into account in the new normal setting such as the environment of the learners, their connectivity to the internet, their individual abilities to learn and digest learnings and their attitude towards communication in a virtual way.

Assessment of tasks varies depending on the lessons presented as well as to the interest of the students. Traditional way of evaluating or assessing their performance may help in a way to help them boost their confidence both in the writing and oral activities and feeding them with information that would help develop their critical thinking skills and become good communicators in ESL. Reinforcement tasks may contribute towards excellent and friendly competition among the learners through participating in collaborative activities, patience and hard work to facilitate a smooth flow of interaction between and among the learners. Harry Wong retorts that "in an effective classroom, students should not only know what they are doing. They should also know why and how."

Time is the essence of teaching and learning. Reducing anxiety does not happen overnight. Students themselves have to try to seek chances to practice using/speaking the language in various situations. Teaching time is limited hence, students need to actively practice the language in and out of the classroom. Sharing their experiences with other students and ESL/EFL teachers is useful to understand the issues of anxiety and fear in different perspectives.

Other approaches to be utilized in the ESL classroom involve students' responses crucial to the quality of the learning experiences. This will greatly depend upon the resourcefulness and creativity of the teacher. There is no 'best' strategy or approach however if one decides to adapt such teaching tool, there must be motivation in the implementation of such strategies to encourage students' motivation by not being a passive or reluctant recipients of knowledge transformation. Strategies or pedagogies are ingredients in teaching. They add colorful flavor to inspire teachers' instructional mode. Although strategies vary, ESL teachers still depend on the learners' interests. No strategy is best as long as it is student-based. Teaching without assessing students' needs is not teaching at all. The real and fundamental core of teaching-learning process builds relationships with students by knowing their strengths. Out of those strategies, students will be motivated to learn and they would eventually participate or perform and be responsible for their own learning.

Native speakers as well as non-native speakers of ESL are in the right track to determine their students intelligibility and accuracy of language use. It applies to both Standard British English or Standard American English. Code-switching and code-mixing usually occurs. In language teaching, there are pedagogical facets that affect the behavior and teaching styles of an ESL educator. Teaching grammar is one. As David Wilkins put it, "Without grammar, very little can be conveyed, without vocabulary, nothing can be conveyed." Some students (if not most) find grammar a tedious yet a boring lesson. Rules introduced repetitively does not offer a 'special flavor' and mastery of the rules seems to be an experience to a lesser extent particularly for those whose field of discipline is not in English. Mixing different languages and switching into another language in an oral discourse has not become a novelty in today's classroom of modern teaching. One of the reasons is the lack of vocabulary or appropriate choice of words that would substitute a specific term. One has to replace for a word or a phrase to complete the meaning of the written discourse.

To facilitate learning, the teacher must learn to match appropriate tasks with students' abilities and background knowledge. When tasks are under estimated, too many students do not learn up to their potentials and get bored (Boisier, 2000). The teachers' attitude and their strategy in teaching ESL is of crucial importance. Tejero (2009) remarked that given all the best in terms of the instructional requirements, teaching and learning may still fall short of the desired expectations if the teacher is not judicious in establishing the right environment for learning. The establishment of a favorable classroom atmosphere which is conducive to effective teaching and learning activities is an essential condition that has to be looked into by any seasoned and perceptive teacher.

By all means, ESL teaching and learning promotes and utilize intellectual understanding of the grammar of the language in real communication. If teachers expect their students to learn how to use language to fulfill real communicative functions, they must have opportunities to do so in a full range of real situations and social settings.

"Learning" occurs as a result of conscious study of the formal properties of the second language. Learning is developed. It is taught by explicit or formal instruction, and it is to be aided by the practice of error correction. In everyday language, acquisition is correct mental representation of a rule. "Learn" knowledge is available for use by "picking up" a language while learning is "grammar" or "rules." It is an accepted truth that being proficient in English is an advantage. It essentially helps a person to articulate his views and express himself and it also enables him/her to excel in a number of specialized fields (Longcop, 2000). Similarly, in order for an individual to succeed in his undertaking, he must have an adequate English language proficiency.

The bedrock of Teaching

Liakoupolou (2011) asserted that knowledge on every subject in the curriculum the teacher teaches is a necessity. Manginsay (2015) too, emphasized that teachers' effectiveness on the subject matter is crucial since it is an indicator that they have a sense of direction and aware of the expected outcomes. Similarly Darling-Hammond (2005) underscored that a teacher needs the kind of knowledge that will enable her to observe her students, assess their attitude and performance so that she can choose those techniques and strategies that are suitable.

It is indeed a requirement that the acquisition of knowledge and skills is connected to the subject being taught. In fact, Duangon (2013) claimed that one indicator of educational excellence is the presence of highly effective, truly committed, and competent classroom teachers. Also, the teacher should be able to bring the updated knowledge to the classroom and should have the expertise to impart it (Bite, 2012). Precisely, the teacher does not only give inspiration and facilitate the learning process but also helps students become better learners. Their excellence and determination in learning depends much on the quality of teaching.

Teacher's effectiveness of teaching the language was a composition of other aspects of instruction in basic classroom that was perceived as sufficient and effective. Focusing on the learner's needs, making the classroom a 'friendly-learning site provides language input and output at an appropriate level. The initial challenge of ESL teachers is the acquisition of skills needed to present and navigate their everyday lessons.

To sum up, ESL teachers of today are not merely provider of lessons in the classroom but they possess some attributes like proficiency in the subject and devotion to the profession. Their success in teaching holds their beliefs that students' good performance usually dwells on how they perform their classroom tasks. It can be assumed that students' failure to understand the topic may result to teacher's inability to elaborate the content. Lack of preparation and interest in the subject may also result to different consequences hence; students are the primary victims of classroom injustice. Teachers' negative attitude toward the students may affect their teaching and certainly failure may occur. Teachers' personal problems too may contribute to the learning difficulty of the students thus resulting to the latter's disinterest in their studies.

Psyche of ESL Teachers

ESL teachers as agents in the classroom are not "information providers" but they should engage in reflection to discover their everyday practices which are fundamental in teaching. Their reflection determines their teaching practices which are fundamental in teaching. Their reflection determines their teaching practice which greatly affects their students' performance. However, being reflective also concerns how they project their image toward their students. Their personal attributes may drive them to acknowledge the unconventional behavior of the students and thus they need to embrace positive characteristics that would boost their morale.

Reflection captures a new picture in the teachers' teaching practices. It provides a link as an initial preparation for them to revise any unexpected outcomes regarding information, students' interests and limitations. Through reflection, one can determine positive changes in his or her teaching journey and it helps him or her enhance his or her actual performance.

Indeed, actual teaching practices produce different techniques that eventually transform individuals to engage in meaningful learning activities. With this, teaching and learning is an on-going challenge that both ESL teachers and students experience both inside the classroom and beyond. Practices are regarded as teaching tools that identify one's profession and lead students to learn in the real world.

Reflective teaching is knowing and understanding the learners. Students deserve what is best for them. In the same light, teachers are challenged to teach thus improving their craft would benefit their students to learn. Reflective teaching is beneficial not only to the teachers but also to the students. It helped them to adjust their instructional goals and objectives based on students' results or responses in learning. They also perceived reflective practice as a preparation for evaluating their teaching, examining their students' learning, and thinking critically and deeply about approaches to improving classroom instruction.

Reflecting is embracing change. Knowing and understanding their students and their needs, the development of their teaching instruction, the use of instructional strategies, and the learning outcomes were the focus of their reflection in teaching.

Moreover, reflections vary and flexibility in teaching occurs anytime in the teaching practice. Doing this provided them the way to evaluate both their students' performance and the results of their teaching which enabled them to ponder or contemplate various approaches for future instruction. Van Manen cited in Disu (2017) considered this as 'contextual reflection.' In this stage, they determine the importance of a lesson based on their students' needs. Learning how to carry out the desired learning goals and modification of instructional mode offers a relaxing climate tension-free classroom. The way in which a teacher carries out his or her work determined by the union or connection of his acquired knowledge and personality traits.

In sum, teachers overall psyche is a component of *understanding and knowing the students, being innovative, selfless, and ready to embrace change.* Therefore, achieving competencies in teaching require such skills that would transform better individuals.

> Decades of education research support the idea that by teaching less and providing more feedback, we can produce greater learning. - Grant Wiggins

At present, she is handling Philippine English, Critical Writing, Introduction to the English Language System, Teaching and Assessment of the Macro-Skills, and Language and Gender courses. Likewise, she is the Instruction and Bachelor of Arts in English Language (BAEL) Program Coordinator.

References

1.   Bernardo, Allan B.I. and Marianne M. Gaerlan. *Non-native English students learning in English: Reviewing and reflecting on the research.* De la Salle University, Philippines.

2.   Boiser, Diosdada C. (2000). Strategies for Teaching. A Modular Application. Manila Philippines. Rex Book Store.

3.   Disu, Abimbola (2017). A Phenomenological Study on Reflective Teaching. Unpublished Dissertation. Concordia University, Portland.

4.   Duangon, Matilde (2013). The teachers' pedagogical approaches and its grammar and oral proficiency. Unpublished Master's thesis. Cebu Normal University. Cebu City.

5.   Dulay, H. and M. Burt (1982). Creative Construction in Second Language Learning and Teaching. Oxford, New York: Oxford University Press.

6.   Liu, Meihua (2005). *Strategies to reduce anxiety in ESL/EFL classroom.*Vol. 27. No. 2.

7.   Longcop, Leonila A. (2000). Narrative Writing in Ninorte Samarnon and English. Its Implications for Second Language/Writing Pedagogy. Unpublished Master's Thesis. University of Eastern Philippines, University Town, Catarman, N. Samar.

8.   Mangada Gladys G. (2018). English Teachers' Reflective Teaching Competence. Unpublished Dissertation. Cebu Normal University. Cebu City.

9.   Olshtain, Elite, et al. (1990). *Factors predicting success in EFL among culturally different learners*. Language Learning. Vol. 40. No.1.

10.   Tejero, Erlinda G. (2009). Multi-disciplinary Teaching Strategies. University of Eastern Philippines.

Author's bio

Professor **Gladys Gayola Mangada** has been working as an Associate Professor of English and a full-time English teacher at the College of Arts and Communication, Department of Languages and Communication University of Eastern Philippines. (UEP) She has attended a number of conferences and seminars in Philippines as well as in abroad. English Pedagogies and Language Learning are her chief area of interest regarding research. She occupies a number of prominent positions, including coordinator of Bachelor of Art in English language (BAEL) programme coordination. She also handles Philippine English critical writing, introduction to the English language system, Teaching and Assessment of macro-skills and gender courses.

N. Lazebna / D. Kumar (Ed.), Studies in Modern English, Würzburg, 2022, p. 81-104. DOI: 10.25972/WUP-978-3-95826-199-0-81

Blended Learning in the New Normal: EFL Student and Teacher Perceptions and Reactions

Md. Maniruzzaman[*]

Abstract

To reopen educational institutions and return to the classroom, we all need to modify how we act to successfully face the challenges of the new normal resulting from the COVID-19 pandemic and entailing our insights into and the after-effects of the pandemic. More specifically, the new normal might encompass online education we are getting used to during the pandemic and the age-old onsite education as well. Thoughtfully integrated, online and onsite learning combine to create blended learning. However, the pertinent literature reveals that English as a foreign language (EFL) students and teachers differently perceive and react to blended learning in diverse contexts. This study was designed to explore student and teacher perceptions of and reactions to blended learning in the Department of English, Jahangirnagar University in the new normal. Fifty undergraduates of EFL and eight teachers of the department participated in the study. To collect data from them, the Student Questionnaire and the Teacher Questionnaire were used. And the data were processed by applying the SPSS programme module. The findings revealed that the majority of the students and the teachers had mostly positive perceptions of blended learning, although the former did not have sufficient exposure to online learning and the latter lacked adequate insights into online teaching. Further, both the students and the teachers expressed mostly positive reactions to blended learning in the new normal, though the former deemed online examinations inadequately smooth and reliable, and the latter had insufficient experience of online instruction and assessment. The study categorically recommends reforming the curriculum, adopting relevant instructional strategies, developing suitable materials, customizing the assessment, integrating and installing technology, training the teachers, upskilling the students for blended learning, improving the infrastructure, and adjusting the management.

Keywords: new normal, blended learning, undergraduates of EFL and teachers, perceptions, reactions

Introduction

We all have been moved, affected, shut down and altered due to the COVID-19 pandemic. Just opening the doors is not sufficient to get back to the classroom. Besides, we all have

---

[*]   PhD, Professor, Department of English, Jahangirnagar University Savar, Dhaka, Bangladesh.

individually changed, and our practices, priorities, needs, interests, and expectations have dramatically shifted. The things that were significant two years ago can appear quite different to what we consider important now. Since we have begun to reopen educational institutions and re-enter the classroom, we all have to adaptthe way we work to fulfil the requirements of the new normal with a conspicuous vision of what the future mightbe like. This is a mode which commences with clarifying and understanding the exact appearance of the new normal. And the new normal will, most probably, accommodate what we are getting used to during the COVID-19 pandemic, that is, emergency remote teaching and online learning plus the age-old in-person learning of English as a foreign language (EFL).

Instruction designed, developed and delivered technologically can meet learner needs and be tailored to the factors individual learners have. Thoughtful planning and development principles and parameters are possibly clear to fully capable students and, meanwhile, allow them with disabilities to have the same educational knowledge and skill (Abernathy, 2001). Alessi and Trollip (1991) identify specific instances in which computer-based teaching proves effective. While some desire some educational experience to be fulfilling to learners, some others also desire to exploit technology maximally to provide for a better learning experience (Dobbs, 2000; Dooling, 2000). As a result, EFL students and teachers might have diverse perceptions of and reactions to blending together online and onsite learning resulting in blended learning.

The worldwide shutdowns of educational institutions caused by the COVID-19 pandemic have substituted in-person education with online teaching and learning traditionally accepted as less demanding, less motivational, less valid, less reliable and less prestigious. The transition to online teaching and learning at lightning speed might have negatively impacted upon student and teacher attitude, motivation, preparedness, practice, and performance, especially in in the Department of English, Jahangirnagar University. Consequently, EFL student and teacher perceptions of and reactions to online teaching and learning might have a bearing on instruction, assessment, and learning outcomes. Moreover, the new normal anticipated as a consequence of the COVID-19 pandemic might demand new plans and policies to implement EFL programmes. Amalgamated, online and onsite learning constitute blended learning. In other words, blended learning incorporates the thoughtful integration of in-person face-to-face learning with online learning (Garrison & Kanuka, 2004). This mode of learning requiring an intentional and integrated approach (Zenger & Uehlein, 2001) encompasses the best practices of online learning and onsite instruction with a view to facilitating learning and should mainly depend upon the needs and interests of students and teachers.

As is observed in the Western World and North America in particular, an English language programme might be a combination of onsite and online education generally termed 'blended or hybrid learning' (Zenger & Uehlein, 2001) in the new normal in many institutions including ours. However, a literature review reveals diverse perceptions and reactions of EFL students and teachers to blended learning in variedsettings (e.g., Wiffin, 2002, Wingard, 2004, Neumeier, 2005, Grgurovic, 2011, @DreamBox_Learn, 2013, O'Connell, 2016, The County Schools, 2021). Moreover, the present researcher was not aware of any such investigations already carried out in Bangladesh, especially in the Department of English, Jahangirnagar University. As the issue remained under-researched, particularly in the

Department of English, Jahangirnagar University, investigations into it were obviously warranted. Hence, the aim of the current study was to examine EFL student and teacher perceptions of and reactions to blended learning in the Department of English, Jahangirnagar University in the new normal.

Literature review

Blended learning has been the focus of many investigations that examined its use and effectiveness in the second/foreign language context. A study conducted by Sharma and Barrett (2007) revealed a number of factors affecting the uptake of blended learning. The factors included positive or negative attitudes of teachers to using technology, learner proficiency, teacher training, and teacher and student accessibility to technology. The factors played an important role in decisions as to carrying out a blended learning approach in English language learning and teaching. Further, Shih (2010) conducted a study with 40 English as a second language learners and unfolded blended learning could be employed productively to enhance learners' language skills. Specifically, the findings showed that the use of the blended learning along with video-based blogs is of benefit including developing the students' speaking skills, improving a sense of independence and collaboration, and promoting learning.

Grgurovic (2011) examined the use of blended learning in an English as a second language setting. The study was planned to ascertain how blended learning was exploited in classes as well as how face-to-face and distance learning were combined. The investigation was carried out in a class offering instruction in speaking and listening in a programme in the USA. The samples were 19 English as a second language students and one English language instructor. The findings showed that blended learning could be productively employed to teach all the language skills. The teachers as well as the students had positive perceptions of and attitudes to incorporating blended learning into teaching English language. The subjects believed that online teaching assisted the traditional ways and hence accelerated the students' language learning. In addition, based on the findings of the study, Marsh (2012) claimed blended learning more effective than traditional teaching in several respects, such as fostering language learners' autonomy, supplying more individualized language support, enhancing collaborative learning, promoting student interaction and participation, facilitating practice of the language skills beyond the classroom, and improving the learners' language skills. Therefore, the purpose of using a blended learning approach can be to find a consistent balance between online access to information and knowledge and onsite activities and interaction.

Manan et al. (2012) investigated the usefulness of teaching in blended learning by using Facebook groups together with face-to-face instruction in an English as a second language context. The study included 30 undergraduate English as a second language learners at a public Malaysian university. The students received instruction through the conventional classroom teaching and Facebook groups as well. It was disclosed that the majority of subjects indicated positive perceptions of the learning strategy. Similarly, Liu (2013) explored the usefulness of blended learning in an English writing course at a university in Beijing.

The investigation evaluated several facets of blended learning including course design, material presentation, student involvement, and classroom assessment. It offered many advantages covering encouraging autonomous learning, promoting classroom interactions, reducing communication anxiety, and developing learners' writing competencies. It was concluded that the use of blended learning was more motivating and inspiriting than only onsite learning.

Ja'ashan (2015) examined student perceptions of and attitudes to blended learning in an English course at Bisha University, Saudi Arabia. A population of 130 undergraduate English learners was surveyed to assess their perceptions and attitudes. The findings of the study showed that students had positive perceptions of blended learning. The subjects believed the blended learning approach could be used to promote their language skills, foster their learning autonomy, accelerate student-teacher interaction, promote the learning process, and help them have interesting learning experiences. Likewise, Banditvilai (2016) carried out a study to examine the use of blended learning to develop learners' English language skills and independence at an Asian university. The research conducted in an English for specific purpose class included 60 undergraduates majoring in English. The results disclosed that the an online approach consistent with classroom instruction improved the English language skills of the language learners. It was also found that blended learning could be used effectively to promote independent learning and learner motivation. The conclusion of the study includes "Blended learning is a valuable concept that can be used to more successfully achieve teaching goals." (p.227).

Ghazizadeh and Fatemipour (2017) explored the impact of using blended learning on enhancing English language learners' reading skills. The subjects were randomly assigned to an experimental group receiving classroom instructions and blended learning, and a control group having a traditional approach to teaching English language. The groups were tested before as well as after the treatment to assess the learners' reading proficiency level. Then using a t-test, the researchers noticed the use of blended learning had a statistically significantly positive impact on the EFL learners' reading proficiency. The investigators also stated that blended learning facilitated the learning and could be productively adopted for teaching English reading. Similarly, a study carried out by Zhang and Zhu (2018) explored the usefulness of blended learning compared to the traditional ways exploited to teach English in China. A sample of 5376 students enrolled in English as a second language courses at a university in Beijing participated in the study. The findings disclosed that the students using a blended learning mode had better achievement in English as a second language courses when compared with other students taught using the traditional classroom methods. Another study conducted by Akbarov, et al. (2018) investigated 162 English language learners' attitudes to blended learning in an EFL context and also revealed the learners' positive perceptions and attitudes regarding blended learning. The findings indicated that the subjects believed that the use of blended learning helped develop their proficiency in English.

Rerung (2018) designed a study to determine 30 students' perceptions of the use of both online and onsite learning in the listening and speaking classroom. The findings of the study disclosed that the majority of the students considered online learning as an alternative tool to assist them in learning. Erickson (2019) carried out a study to examine blended learning in Adult Basic Education ESL programmes because it develops as a new practice. Data were collected from 11 Adult Basic Education English teachers of the United States by using in-depth interviews. The study revealed that the ESL educational setting was unique in ways that influenced how blended learning should have been used.

To conclude, the study reviewed above uncovered that blended learning can be employed to promote the learning process and achieving learning outcomes. EFL learners usually have positive perceptions of and attitudes to blended learning as teaching mode. The positive perspectives are derived from several directions covering enhancing students' language skills in an interacting and engaging context, facilitating the learning, and creating opportunities to be autonomous learners.

Research Questions

To achieve the objectives of the current study, the following research questions were formulated:

RQ1: How do the EFL students of the Department of English, Jahangirnagar University perceive blended learning in the new normal?

RQ2: What are the reactions of the EFL students of the Department of English, Jahangirnagar University to blended learning in the new normal?

RQ3: How do the EFL teachers of the Department of English, Jahangirnagar University view blended learning in the new normal?

RQ4: What are the reactions of the EFL teachers of the Department of English, Jahangirnagar University to blended learning in the new normal?

Method

Respondents

Fifty undergraduates of EFL and eight teachers of the Department of English, Jahangirnagar University randomly selected responded to the respective questionnaires. Random samplings are usually strongly preferred since all populations possess the same possibility to be selected and can easily be calculated in an investigation. Hence, the present study exploited the simple random sampling while selecting the respondents because it was easy to apply, inexpensive and caused comparatively less trouble (Robert, 1997).

Instruments

To collect data from 50 undergraduates of EFL and eight teachers of the Department of English, Jahangirnagar University, the Student Questionnaire (Appendix-I) and the Teacher Questionnaire (Appendix-II) were used. The questionnaires were modelled on the scale and questionnaire developed by Albirini (2006), Al-Zaiydeen et al. (2010), the questionnaire and focus group discussions employed by Khan, et al., (2021), and semi-structured interviews designed by Agboola (2016). Both questionnaires were concerned with two major variables – student/teacher perceptions of and reactions to blended learning.

Student perceptions of blended learning related to the first research question "How do the students of the Department of English, Jahangirnagar University perceive hybrid learning in the new normal?" entailed six items, Question No. 11 to 16, covering aware of best practices of onsite learning, aware of best practices of online learning, online delivery being more attractive and effective than onsite, onsite activities being more attractive and effective than online, teachers enjoying onsite plus online teaching more, and a thoughtful combination of online and onsite learning more.

Similarly, teacher perceptions of blended learning linked to the third research question "How do the teachers of the Department of English, Jahangirnagar University view hybrid learning in the new normal?" included six items, Question No. 11 to 16, encompassing aware of best practices of onsite learning, aware of best practices of online learning, online delivery being more attractive and effective than onsite, onsite activities being more attractive and effective than online, students enjoying onsite plus online teaching more, and a thoughtful combination of online and onsite learning more.

Again, student reactions to blended learning concerned with the second research question "What are the reactions of the students of the Department of English, Jahangirnagar University to hybrid learning in the new normal?" had 10 items, Question No. 1 to 10, including student readiness, student interest, student feeling of teacher motivation, and student capability.

Likewise, teacher reactions to blended learning connected with the fourth research question "What are the reactions of the teachers of the Department of English, Jahangirnagar University to hybrid learning in the new normal?" entailed 10 items, Question No. 1 to 10, covering teacher readiness, teacher interest, teacher feeling of student motivation, and teacher expertise.

Thus, each of the questionnaires included 16 items designed as the 5-point scale (Likert, 1932), in which 1=strongly disagree, 2=disagree, 3=undecided, 4=agree, and 5=strongly agree.

Collection and Analysis of Data

The data for the current study were collected from two populations – one including 50 undergraduates of EFL and the other consisting eight teachers of the Department of English, Jahangirnagar University by using the Student Questionnaire and the Teacher Questionnaire respectively. Fifty undergraduates of EFL and eight teachers of the Department of

English, Jahangirnagar University responded to the respective questionnaires online. The usable response rate of the students was 83% and that of the teachers was 62%. The data collected from the students and the teachers were processed and analyzed by operating the Statistical Package for Social Science (SPSS) programme module. More specifically, descriptive statistics were employed to sum up the data including frequency percentages, means and standard deviations.

Findings and Discussion

The findings of the analysis of the data collected from both student and teacher respondents have been presented below according to their responses to different variables constituting the research questions related to their perceptions of and reactions to blended learning during the new normal.

RQ1: How do the students of the Department of English, Jahangirnagar University perceive blended learning in the new normal?

Student perceptions of blended learning in the new normal included six items, Item No. 11 to 16, awareness of best practices of onsite learning, awareness of best practices of online learning, online delivery being more attractive and effective than onsite, onsite activities being more attractive and effective than online, teachers enjoying onsite plus online teaching more, and a thoughtful combination of online and onsite learning being more effective than online or onsite learning alone.

The findings of descriptive analysis showed that 90% students (Strongly Agree 34% + Agree 56%) were aware of best practices of onsite learning, whereas 48% students (Strongly Agree 12% + Agree 36%) were aware of best practices of online learning and 34% did not have any opinion.

Further, 36% students (Strongly Agree 8% + Agree 28%) considered online content delivery more attractive and effective than onsite delivery, but 36% did not, whereas 28% expressed no views. On the other hand, 84% students were in favor of onsite activities being more attractive and effective than online activities.

Again, 68% students (Strongly Agree 22% + Agree 46%) felt their teachers were enjoying onsite plus online teaching more than only onsite or online teaching. And 80% students (Strongly Agree 48% + Agree 32%) supported a thoughtful combination of online and onsite teaching being more effective than online or onsite learning alone.

Thus, the majority of the students of the Department of English, Jahangirnagar University positively perceived hybrid learning in the new normal, although only 48% students were aware of best practices of online learning and only 36% students considered online content delivery more attractive and effective than onsite delivery. The findings were consistent with the Means 4.16, 3.32, 2.98, 4.24, 3.74 and 4.16 and Standard Deviations .842, 1.115, 1.134, .716, 1.065 and 1.017 respectively (Table 5.1.1.1).

		Aware of best practices of onsite learning	Aware of best practices of online learning	Online delivery more attractive and effective than onsite	Onsite activities more attractive and effective than online	Teachers enjoying onsite plus online teaching more	A thoughtful combination of online and onsite learning more
N	Valid	50	50	50	50	50	50
	Missing	0	0	0	0	0	0
Mean		4.16	3.32	2.98	4.24	3.74	4.16
Median		4.00	3.00	3.00	4.00	4.00	4.00
Mode		4	4	3[a]	4	4	5
Std. Deviation		.842	1.115	1.134	.716	1.065	1.017
Minimum		1	1	1	3	1	2
Maximum		5	5	5	5	5	5

Table 5.1.1.1: Student perceptions of hybrid learning

To discuss the findings presented above, it is conspicuous that the first research question "How do the students of the Department of English, Jahangirnagar University perceive hybrid learning in the new normal?" received mixed responses from the students. First, 90% students were aware of best practices of onsite learning, but only 48% students were aware of best practices of online learning and 34% did not have any opinion. The findings are indicative of the scenario that the students were already used to traditional age-old onsite learning but recently began to receive online instruction and take online examinations through emergency remote teaching just after the start of COVID-19 pandemic in Bangladesh in March 2020. Second, only 36% students considered online content delivery more attractive and effective than onsite delivery, but 36% did not, whereas 28% expressed no view. The findings indicate the students' inadequate exposure to online education because it abruptly started due to the COVID-19 pandemic in March 2020. On the contrary, 84% students preferred onsite activities to online activities since they were traditionally involved in face-to-face onsite education. Third, 68% students found their teachers enjoying onsite plus online teaching more than only onsite or online teaching, and 80% favored a thoughtful combination of online and onsite teaching as being more effective than only online or onsite learning.

Thus, the students of the Department of English, Jahangirnagar University had mostly positive perceptions of blended learning, an intended and integrated mixture of onsite and online learning. These findings lend support to the findings of the studies conducted by Manan et al. (2012), Ja'ashan (2015), Banditvilai (2016), Ghazizadeh and Fatemipour (2017), Zhang and Zhu (2018), Akbarov, et al. (2018) and the like.

RQ2: What are the reactions of the students of the Department of English, Jahangirnagar University to blended learning in the new normal?

Student reactions to blended learning in the new normal covered 10 items, Item No. 1 to 10, preparedness for online learning, readiness for onsite learning, online learning orientation, onsite learning orientation, being interested in online learning, being interested in onsite learning, no difficulty with teachers in online classes, no difficulty with teachers in onsite classes, feeling confident and comfortable to learn online and onsite, and taking online examinations smoothly and reliably.

Firstly, descriptive analysis revealed that 82% students (Strongly Agree 14% + Agree 68%) were prepared for online learning, and 88% students (Strongly Agree 46% + Agree 42%) were ready for onsite learning. Again, 52% students (Strongly Agree 10% + Agree 42%) had online learning orientation while 90% students (Strongly Agree 36% + Agree 54%) had onsite learning orientation.

That is, most of the students of the Department of English, Jahangirnagar University were ready for both online and onsite learning combined to design hybrid learning. Besides, the majority of the students had both online and onsite learning orientation though they were more used to traditional onsite than online learning. The findings were in harmony with the Means 3.88, 4.30, 3.30, and 4.14 and Standard Deviations .773, .814, 1.093 and .969 respectively (Table 5.1.2.1).

		Preparedness for online learning	Readiness for onsite learning	Online learning orientation	Onsite learning orientation
N	Valid	50	50	50	50
	Missing	0	0	0	0
Mean		3.88	4.30	3.30	4.14
Median		4.00	4.00	4.00	4.00
Mode		4	5	4	4
Std. Deviation		.773	.814	1.093	.969
Minimum		1	1	1	1
Maximum		5	5	5	5

Table 5.1.2.1: Student readiness for onsite and online learning

Secondly, 78% students (Strongly Agree 28% + Agree 50%) were interested in online learning and 90% students (Strongly Agree 52% + Agree 38%) were for onsite learning.

That is to say, the vast majority of the students of the Department of English, Jahangirnagar University were interested in both online and onsite learning thoughtfully blended to produce hybrid or blended learning. The results were in consonance with the Means 3.92 and 4.38 and Standard Deviations 1.007 and .805 respectively (Table 5.1.2.2).

		Interested in online learning	Interested in onsite learning
N	Valid	50	50
	Missing	0	0
Mean		3.92	4.38
Median		4.00	5.00
Mode		4	5
Std. Deviation		1.007	.805
Minimum		1	1
Maximum		5	5

Table 5.1.2.2: Student interest in online and onsite learning

		No difficulty with teachers in online classes	No difficulty with teachers in onsite classes
N	Valid	50	50
	Missing	0	0
Mean		3.22	3.62
Median		4.00	4.00
Mode		4	4
Std. Deviation		1.093	1.159
Minimum		1	1
Maximum		5	5

Table 5.1.2.3: Teacher feeling of student motivation

Thirdly, 54% students (Strongly Agree 4% + Agree 50%) encountered no difficulty with their teachers in online learning and 66% students (Strongly Agree 20% + Agree 46%) faced no difficulty with their teachers in onsite learning.

In other words, most of the students of the Department of English, Jahangirnagar University did not confront any difficulty with their teachers both in online and onsite learning purposefully mixed to generate hybrid learning. The findings agreed with the Means 3.22 and 3.62 and Standard Deviations 1.093 and 1.159 respectively (Table 5.1.2.3).

Fourthly, 72% students (Strongly Agree 22% + Agree 50%) confidently and comfortably learned online and onsite as well and only 40% students (Strongly Agree 8% + Agree 32%) smoothly and reliably took online examinations, whereas 44% students (Strongly Disagree 14%+ Disagree 30%) did not.

That is, most of the students of the Department of English, Jahangirnagar University were confident and comfortable both in online and onsite learning. Nonetheless, a large number of students (44%) could not take online examinations smoothly and reliably. The findings matched the Means 3.76 and 2.90 and Standard Deviations 1.061 and 1.233 respectively (Table 5.1.2.3).

To respond to the second research question "What are the reactions of the students of the Department of English, Jahangirnagar University to hybrid learning in the new normal?", it is found that the students expressed mostly positive attitudes and feelings. Firstly, most of the were students ready for both online and onsite learning with relatively more traditional onsite learning orientation. The finding might be attributed to the reality of the students attending age-old face-to-face classes. Secondly, the large majority of the students had interest in both online and onsite learning together resulting in hybrid learning. This is because of the fact that the students had already had experience of in-person learning and then started to have additional experience of online learning happening during the COVID-19 pandemic. Thirdly, more than 50% students did not face any difficulty with their teachers both in online and onsite learning purposively blended to design hybrid learning. This finding again indicates positive attitudes to both face-to-face and virtual learning and is in harmony with the previous findings. Fourthly, most of the students (72%) felt confident and comfortable both in online and onsite learning, a large number of them (44%) could not take online assessments smoothly and reliably. This finding might be attributed to their new and inadequate experience of online assessments quite different from onsite examinations. The positive reactions of the students to hybrid learning during the new normal countenance the findings of the research conducted by Shih (2010), Grgurovic (2011), Liu (2013), Ja'ashan (2015), Akbarov, et al. (2018) and so forth.

		Confident and comfortable to learn online and onsite	Taking online examinations smoothly and reliably
N	Valid	50	50
	Missing	0	0
Mean		3.76	2.90
Median		4.00	3.00
Mode		4	4
Std. Deviation		1.061	1.233
Minimum		1	1
Maximum		5	5

Table 5.1.2.4: Student capability of learning online and onsite and taking examinations online

RQ3: How do the teachers of the Department of English, Jahangirnagar University view blended learning in the new normal?

Teacher perceptions of blended learning in the new normal encompassed six items, Item No. 11 to 16, awareness of best practices of onsite learning, awareness of best practices of online learning, online delivery being more attractive and effective than onsite, onsite activities being more attractive and effective than online, students enjoying onsite plus online teaching more, and a thoughtful combination of online and onsite learning being more effective than only online or onsite learning.

The results of descriptive analysis disclosed that all the teachers (Strongly Agree 100% and Strongly Agree 75% + Agree 25% respectively) were aware of best practices of onsite learning as well as online learning.

Next, 50% teachers (Strongly Agree 50%) opined that online content delivery was more attractive and effective than onsite delivery, whereas 50% of them (Strongly Disagree 25% + Disagree 25%) expressed as an opposite view on the factor. Besides, 75% teachers (Strongly Agree 75%) considered onsite activities more attractive and effective than online activities.

Moreover, 50% teachers (Strongly Agree 25% + Agree 25%) felt that their students were enjoying onsite plus online teaching more than onsite or online alone while 50% of them gave no opinion. Further, 100% teachers (Strongly Agree 50% + Agree 50%) were in favor of a thoughtful combination of online and onsite teaching being more effective than only online or onsite learning.

Hence, most of the teachers of the Department of English, Jahangirnagar University had positive perceptions of hybrid or blended learning in the new normal. These results were consistent with the Means 5.00, 4.50, 3.25, 4.50, 3.75 and 4.50 and Standard Deviations .000, .926, 1.909, .926, .886 and .535 respectively.

To discuss the results displayed and described above, the teachers expressed their positive views on the third research question "How do the teachers of the Department of English, Jahangirnagar University view hybrid learning in the new normal?". First, 100% teachers were aware of best practices of both onsite learning and online learning combined to create hybrid learning. This was because of the teachers' regular involvement in age-old face-to-face education and their conducting online classes and assessments during the COVID-19 pandemic that started in Bangladesh in March 2020. Second, 50% teachers thought that online content delivery was more attractive and effective than onsite delivery, whereas 50% of them did not. Further, 75% teachers preferred onsite activities being more attractive and effective than online activities. The findings unfold the teachers' insufficient knowledge and practice of online education which was new to them as they started working with this mode of instruction just after the beginning of the COVID-19 pandemic that started in Bangladesh in March 2020. Third, 50% teachers felt that their students were enjoying onsite plus online teaching more than only onsite or online, whereas 50% teachers expressed no opinion. However, 100% teachers supported a thoughtful combination of online and onsite teaching being more effective than online or onsite teaching in isolation.

Hence, most of the teachers of the Department of English, Jahangirnagar University had positive perceptions of hybrid or blended learning in the new normal, although they appeared to have inadequate insight into online learning and teaching. The findings lend support to those revealed by the studies carried out by Grgurovic (2011), Marsh (2012). Liu (2013) and so on. In addition, the perceptions the teachers of hybrid learning were consistent with those of the students in the Department of English, Jahangirnagar University.

RQ4: What are the reactions of the teachers of the Department of English, Jahangirnagar University to blended learning in the new normal?

Teacher reactions to blended learning in the new normal included 10 items, Item No. 1 to 10, preparedness for online teaching, readiness for onsite teaching, formal training in online teaching, formal training in onsite teaching, being interested in online teaching, being interested in onsite teaching, no difficulty with students in online classes, no difficulty with students in onsite classes, feeling confident and comfortable to teach online and onsite, and conducting online examinations smoothly and reliably.

Descriptive analysis showed that 100% teachers (Strongly Agree 75% + Agree 25%) were prepared for online teaching, and 100% of them (Strongly Agree 100%) were ready for onsite teaching. Further, only 50% teachers (Strongly Agree 50%, No Opinion 25%, and Strongly Disagree 25%) had formal training in online teaching, and only 50% of them (Strongly Agree 50%, No Opinion 25%, and Strongly Disagree 25%) had formal training in onsite teaching.

Thus, all the teachers of the Department of English, Jahangirnagar University were prepared for both online and onsite teaching integrated into hybrid or blended learning. However, only 50% teachers had formal training in online and onsite teaching. The findings were in consonance with the Means 4.75, 5.00, 3.50, and 3.50 and Standard Deviations .463, .000, 1.773 and 1.773 respectively.

Again, 100% teachers (Strongly Agree 75% + Agree 25%) were interested in online teaching, and 100% teachers (Strongly Agree 100%) also liked onsite teaching. That is, all the teachers of the Department of English, Jahangirnagar University were interested in both online and onsite teaching. These findings agreed with the Means 4.75 and 5.00 and Standard Deviations .463 and .000 respectively.

Furthermore, 75% teachers (Agree 75%, No Opinion 25%) faced no difficulty with their students in online classes and 100% teachers (Strongly Agree 75% + Agree 25%) confronted no difficulty with their students in onsite classes.

Therefore, almost all the teachers of the Department of English, Jahangirnagar University did not encounter any difficulty with their students both in online and onsite classes thoughtfully blended to create hybrid learning. The findings were consistent with the Means 3.75 and 4.75 and Standard Deviations .463 and .463 respectively (Table 5.1.4.3).

Finally, 75% teachers (Strongly Agree 75%, No Opinion 25%) were confident and comfortable both in online and onsite and only 75% teachers (Strongly Agree 50%+ Agree 25%) smoothly and reliably conducted online examinations, while 25% teachers (Disagree 25%) did not.

Hence, a large majority of the teachers of the Department of English, Jahangirnagar University were confident and comfortable in online and onsite teaching as well. Similarly, most of the teachers were capable to conduct online examinations smoothly and reliably. These

		No difficulty with students in online classes	No difficulty with students in onsite classes
N	Valid	8	8
	Missing	0	0
Mean		3.75	4.75
Median		4.00	5.00
Mode		4	5
Std. Deviation		.463	.463
Minimum		3	4
Maximum		4	5

Table 5.1.4.3: Teacher feeling of student motivation

		Confident and comfortable to teach online and onsite	Conducting online examinations smoothly and reliably
N	Valid	8	8
	Missing	0	0
Mean		4.50	4.00
Median		5.00	4.50
Mode		5	5
Std. Deviation		.926	1.309
Minimum		3	2
Maximum		5	5

Table 5.1.4.4: Teacher expertise in teaching onsite and online and conducting examinations online

results agreed with the Means 4.50 and 4.00 and Standard Deviations .926 and 1.309 respectively (Table 5.1.4.3).

The analysis and interpretation of the teachers' reactions to the fourth research question "What are the reactions of the teachers of the Department of English, Jahangirnagar University to hybrid learning in the new normal?" uncover that all the teachers were somewhat prepared for both online and onsite teaching included in hybrid or blended learning, although only half of them were trained in online and onsite teaching. These results were also well-aligned with the teacher's interest in both online and onsite teaching. Further, the teachers did not face any difficulty with their students both in online and onsite classes thoughtfully mixed to design hybrid or blended learning. Besides, two-thirds of the teachers were confident and comfortable in online and onsite teaching and capable to conduct online examinations smoothly and reliably, although 25% teachers had lacked skill at administering online assessment. The findings might be attributed to some factors such as their experience of age-old face-to-face teaching in the classrooms almost without any formal training, and their practice of online instruction and assessment started with an outbreak of the COVID-19 pandemic in Bangladesh in March 2020 and supported by several online webinars and workshops arranged by the university authority.

Therefore, most of the teachers of the Department of English, Jahangirnagar University showed positive reactions to hybrid or blended learning in the new normal, though they seemed to lack sufficient exposure to online instruction and assessment. The results support to those disclosed by the studies carried out by Grgurovic (2011), Marsh (2012). Liu (2013) and so on. In addition, the perceptions the teachers of blended learning were consistent with those of the students in the Department of English, Jahangirnagar University.

Findings in Brief

As the study revealed, the first research question "How do the students of the Department of English, Jahangirnagar University perceive blended learning in the new normal?" received mixed responses from the student respondents. That is, the students had mostly positive perceptions of blended learning, an intended and integrated blend of onsite and online learning, although they seemed to lack sufficient exposure to online learning.

To respond to the second research question "What are the reactions of the students of the Department of English, Jahangirnagar University to blended learning in the new normal?", the students expressed mostly positive attitudes and feelings. That is, the students had mostly positive reactions to blended learning, though they deemed online examinations insufficiently smooth and reliable.

The teachers of the Department of English, Jahangirnagar University positively responded to the third research question "How do the teachers of the Department of English, Jahangirnagar University view blended learning in the new normal?". That is, most of the teachers had positive perceptions of blended learning in the new normal, although they lacked adequate insight into online education.

Finally, the teachers' reactions to the fourth research question "What are the reactions of the teachers of the Department of English, Jahangirnagar University to blended learning in the new normal?" disclosed that all of them were ready for both online and onsite teaching, although only half of them were trained in online and onsite teaching. Therefore, most of the teachers showed positive reactions to blended learning in the new normal, though they did not have sufficient exposure to online instruction and assessment.

Recommendations

Based on the findings summed up above, the study has made recommendations for reforming the curriculum, adopting relevant instructional strategies, developing suitable materials, customizing the assessment system, integrating and installing technology, training the teachers, upskilling the students for hybrid learning, improving the infrastructure, and adjusting the management.

The curriculum already in use for traditional face-to-face education in the classroom in the Department of English, Jahangirnagar university has to be modified and even redesigned to meet the requirements of the blended learning model, for instance, the flipped classroom adopted as suitable for the learners. That is, reformation should include modification and/or redesign of the components of the existing curriculum, such as its visions, missions, program outcomes, course objectives, teaching/learning items, instructional techniques, materials and resources, technology, infrastructure, management and so on. The basic principle controlling blended learning is to orient materials and resources to online delivery and activities and engagement to face-to-face classroom interaction, collaboration, and cooperation.

The instructional strategies, such as pair work, group work, role-plays, simulations, jigsaws and so forth that are especially effective in engaging and supporting learning in students from diverse backgrounds should be adopted. As content is delivered online and activities are performed onsite in blended learning, students should be prepared to receive materials provided by teachers and take preparation for face-to-face classroom activities based on the materials.

To development materials for blended learning, the following actions should be taken step by step: defining the intended learning outcomes of the course, creating an outline for the learning programme, determining the level of interactivity, integrating group collaboration activities, facilitating communication, compiling an inventory of resources to support learning, and making an assessment system. As content is delivered online and tasks are carried out onsite, both soft and printed materials should be prepared, adapted, selected, adopted and/or used.

To align assessment with blended learning, the assessment system of the existing the programme needs to be replanned and customized. That is, the formative assessment, such as quizzes, presentations, assignments, portfolios, viva voce and the like can be administered online while the summative assessment, for example, the course final examinations can be given and taken onsite.

In blended learning, integration of technology is as essential as multi-dimensional. There should be sufficient space and use of necessary technological tools in the curriculum, instructional strategies, materials, and even a single lesson plan. For example, materials should allow teachers to deliver them through online file hosting services like dropbox, google drive, etc. emails, google classroom and so on.

As blended learning entails extensive use of technological tools as well as online operations including basic computer and smart phone literacy, the teachers have to have hands-on training relevant to their instruction and assessment. And the management should arrange required workshops, seminars and the like to train its teachers so that they can comfortably and confidently conduct blended learning.

The students are commonly used to age-old face-to-face learning in the classroom setting. To make them capable of being involved in blended learning, they should be exposed to this new mode of learning through varied orientation and motivational events including workshops, seminars, presentations and so forth. Besides, the management should upskill them and help them acquire basic computer and smartphone literacy.

To implement blended learning, some infrastructural supports are required. The infrastructure covers computers and/or laptops, multi-media projectors, sound systems, interactive whiteboards, Internet connection with adequate speed, sufficient power supply, networking equipment, well-equipped classrooms, digital libraries, management facilities and so forth.

The management including the department Chairperson, teachers, non-academic staff members and technical persons has to adjust itself to blended learning. This is because they are responsible for the different aspects of the blended programme and operation, such as planning the programme encompassing the curriculum, materials, assessment and so on, extending managerial and technical assistance, providing infrastructural and financial support, ensuring training and orientation facilities and the like.

References

1.   @DreamBox_Learn. (2013). 6 models of blended learning. https://www.dreambox.com/blog/6-models-blended-learning

2.   Abernathy, D. J. (2001). @work. *Learning circuits*. http://www.learningcircuits.com/2001/nov2001/@work.html.

3.   Agboola, M. O. (2016). Teacher Attitudes towards Using ICT as an Educational Tool: The Case of Nigerian Secondary School Teachers in the City of Ibadan and Abuja. Master's thesis, Eastern Mediterranean University.

4.   Akbarov, A., Gönen, K., & Aydoğan, H. (2018). Students' attitudes toward blended learning in EFL context. *Acta Didactica Napocensia, 11*(1), 61-68.

5.   Albirini, A. A. (2006). Teacher's attitudes toward information and communication technologies: The case of Syrian EFL teachers. *Journal of Computers and Education, 47*, 373-398.

6.   Alessi, S. M., & Trollip, S. R. (1991). *Computer-based instruction: methods and development*. (2nd ed.). Prentice Hall.

7.   Al-Zaidiyeen, N. J., Leong L. M., & Fong S. F. (2010). Teachers' attitudes and levels of technology use in classrooms: The case of Jordan schools. *International Education Studies, 3*(2). http://www.ccsenet.org/journal/index.php/ies/article/view/5891

8.   Banditvilai, C. (2016). Enhancing students' language skills through blended learning. *Electronic Journal of e-Learning, 14*(3), 220-229.

9.   Dobbs, K. (2000). What the online world needs now: quality. *Training, 37*(9), 84-94.

10.   Dooling, J. O. (2000). What students want to learn about computers. *Educational Leadership, 58*(2), 20-24.

11.   Erickson, B. (2019). Blended learning among adult English as a second language programs. *Culminating Projects in Education Administration and Leadership. 55.* https://repository.stcloudstate.edu/edad_etds/55

12.   Garrison, D. R. & Kanuka, H. (2004). Blended learning: Uncovering its transformative potential in higher education. *The Internet and Higher Education, 7*(2), 95-105.

13.   Ghazizadeh, T., & Fatemipour, H. (2017). The effect of blended learning on EFL learners' reading proficiency. *Journal of Language Teaching and Research, 8*(3), 606-614.

14.   Grgurovic, M. (2011). Blended learning in an ESL Class: A case study. *CALICO Journal, 29* (1),100-117.

15.   Ja'ashan, M. M. (2015). Perceptions and attitudes towards blended learning for English courses: A case study of students at University of Bisha. *English Language Teaching, 8*(9), 40-50.

16.   Khan, R., Basu, B. L., Bashir, A. & Uddin, M. E. (2021). Online instruction during COVID-19 at public universities in Bangladesh: Teacher and student voices. *Teaching English as a Second Language Electronic Journal (TESL-EJ), 25*(1). https://tesl-ej.org/pdf/ej97/a19.pdf

17.   Likert, R. (1932). A Technique for the measurement of attitudes. *Archives of Psychology, 140*, 1–55.

18.   Liu, M. (2013). Blended Learning in a University EFL Writing Course: Description and Evaluation. *Journal of Language Teaching & Research, 4*(2), 301-309.

19.   Manan, N. A. A., Alias, A. A., & Pandian, A. (2012). Utilizing a social networking website as an ESL pedagogical tool in a blended learning environment: An exploratory study. *International Journal of Social Sciences & Education, 2*(1), 1-9.

20.   Marsh, D. (2012). *Blended learning: Creating learning opportunities for language learners.* Cambridge University Press.

21.   Neumeier, P. (2005). A closer look at blended learning: Parameters for designing a blended learning environment for language teaching and learning. *ReCALL, 17*(2), 163-178.

22.   O'Connell, A. (2016). Seven blended learning models used today in higher ed. http://acrobatiq.com/seven-blended-learning-models-used-today-in-higher-ed/

23.   Rerung, M. K. T. (2018). Students' perception on blended learning in English listening and speaking class. *Journal of English Language and Culture, 9*(1), 17–28.

24.   Robert, G. (1997). *Statistical methods for education*. Prentice Hall.

25.   Sharma, P., & Barrett, B. (2007). *Blended learning: Using technology in and beyond the language classroom*. Macmillan education.

26.   Shih, R. C. (2010). Blended learning using video-based blogs: Public speaking for English as a second language students. *Australasian Journal of Educational Technology, 26*(6), 883-897.

27.   The County Schools. (2021). https://www.tiftschools.com/apps/pages/index.jsp?uREC_ID=269041&type=d&pREC_ID=701255

28.   Wiffin, S. (2002). A conceptual framework for K-12 blended instruction design. http://www.pinetree.sd43.bc.ca/teachers/whiffin/papers/K12BlendedDesignModel.pdf.

29.   Wingard, R.G. (2004). Classroom teaching changes in web-enhanced courses: A multi-institutional study. Educause Quarterly, *27*(1), 26-35.

30.   Zenger, J., & Uehlein, C. (2001). Why blended learning will win: The lion and the lamb lie down together. *Training and Development, 55*(8), 55-60.

31.   Zhang, W., & Zhu, C. (2018). Comparing learning outcomes of blended learning and traditional face-to-face learning of university students in ESL courses. *International Journal on E-Learning, 17*(2), 251-273.

Appendix

Appendix-I

The Student Questionnaire

Indicators:

Please consider the scale:

Strongly disagree = SD =1; Disagree = D = 2; No opinion =NO = 3;

Agree =A = 4; Strongly agree = SA =5

Instructions:

Please read the following statements and tick one of the options that best expresses your opinion/feeling/reaction/attitude/experience:

Sl. No.	Item	Opinion				
		SD=1	D=2	NO=3	A=4	SA=5
1	I am prepared to learn English language online.					
2	I am ready to learn English language onsite.					
3	I have online English language learning orientation.					
4	I have onsite English language learning orientation.					
5	I am interested to learn English language online.					
6	I am interested to learn English language onsite.					
7	I face no difficulty with my teachers because they are ready and motivated to conduct online classes.					

8	I face no difficulty with my teachers because they are ready and motivated to conduct onsite classes.					
9	I can confidently and comfortably learn English listening, speaking, reading and writing online and onsite.					
10	I can take online English language examinations smoothly and reliably.					
11	I know onsite English language learning has some best practices.					
12	I know online English language learning has some best practices.					
13	I find online delivery of materials is more attractive and effective than onsite delivery.					
14	I realize onsite activities are more attractive and effective than online activities.					
15	I find my teachers enjoy a combination of onsite and online teaching more than only onsite or online teaching.					
16	I think a thoughtful combination of online and onsite learning will be more effective than online or onsite learning alone.					

Appendix-II

The Teacher Questionnaire

<u>Indicators:</u>
Please consider the scale:
Strongly disagree = SD =1; Disagree = D = 2; No opinion =NO = 3;
Agree =A = 4; Strongly agree = SA =5

<u>Instructions:</u>
Please read the following statements and tick one of the options that best expresses
your perception/opinion/feeling/reaction/attitude/experience:

Sl. No.	Item	Opinion				
		SD=1	D=2	NO=3	A=4	SA=5
1	I am prepared to teach English language online.					
2	I am ready to teach English language onsite.					
3	I have formal training in online English language teaching.					
4	I have formal training in onsite English language teaching.					
5	I am interested to teach English language online.					
6	I am interested to teach English language onsite.					
7	I face no difficulty with my students because they are ready and motivated to attend online classes.					
8	I face no difficulty with my students because they are ready and motivated to attend onsite classes.					

9	I can confidently and comfortably teach English listening, speaking, reading and writing online and onsite.					
10	I can conduct online English language ex-aminations smoothly and reliably.					
11	I am aware of some best practices of on-site English language teaching.					
12	I know online Eng-lish language teach-ing has some best practices.					
13	I understand online delivery of materials is more attractive and effective than onsite delivery.					
14	I feel onsite activities are more attractive and effective than online activities.					
15	I find my students enjoy a combination of onsite and online learning more than only onsite or online learning.					
16	I think a thoughtful combination of online and onsite teaching will be more effective than online or onsite teaching alone.					

Author's bio

Md. Maniruzzaman has been working as a professor, Department of English at Jahangirnagar University, Bangladesh. He is also rendering his services as global professional member of TESOL International Association. He has more than 100 research papers to his credit in reputed National as well as International journals which bear testimony of his scholarship. Besides, he has a contributed immensely in the area of translation, book reviews and books as a sole author. His trust areas of research include TESOL methodology, curriculum and syllabus design, educational technology and management coupled with literatures in English.

N. Lazebna / D. Kumar (Ed.), Studies in Modern English, Würzburg, 2022, p. 105-115. DOI: 10.25972/WUP-978-3-95826-199-0-105

Linguistic Democratization of the Modern English Language: Functional Parameters of English Youth Slang Neologisms

Yuliya Shtaltovna[*]

Due to the extraordinary speed of globalization and technologization, lexical innovations appear anywhere on the planet and almost immediately (if not virally) are used by the entire Internet audience of *homo imitans* as defined by L. Herrero (Herrero, 2011, p.129), they are often augmented by the I-parameter, accurately proving the anthropological dominance of linguistic studies.

Both intralingual and extralingual factors cause the dynamics of the neologism appearance in the language. Being socially and historically determined, innovations can reflect the level of culture, economy, science, education, social differentiation of society, and the dominant ideological trends and views. In contrast, innovations can be indicators of the general psychological state of society and the interaction of ethnic groups. Extralingualism in enriching vocabulary reflects the need to nominate new, relevant concepts of a nation's time or cultural period. A collection of innovations of a particular era of human existence distinguishes the picture of the world of native speakers. Internet (r)-evolution in the first 20 years of the 21st century is replete with "infoneologisms" (Zatsny, 1998, p.174), and "cyberneologisms" (Makhachashvili, 2010, p.217), which cover almost all spheres of life.

Having conducted a quantitative analysis of neologisms recorded by Paul McFedries (McFedries, n.d.) for the last 18 years, namely on August 25, 2013, their number is 5452 units, which are divided into eight spheres of life, we can see that the new units to define society and culture created the most, together this figure is 42% of all neologisms. After conducting a quantitative analysis of neologisms, we found that the newest units for the definition of society and culture created this figure is 42% of all neologisms. The result of dynamics and qualitative changes in synchrony: the first group (8%) comprises terms, jargon, and reactivated lexical units with remarks of size, dialectic vocabulary, the third (6.5) - reactivated lexis and rarely used units, the fourth (15.5%) - lexicalized phrases, as well as established verbal complexes.

N-Gram Viewer can visually show case the peaks of the democratization processes unfolding in humankind's history (Figure 1). The linguistic democratization of the Ukrainian and English languages has been the scope of our research interest since 2006 and 2013, respectively. The linguistic democratization of English influences the processes of word formation in the cultural sphere of life, and perception of the world is studied (Shtaltovna, 2014) with the focus on lexical and semantic processes are distinguished and quantitative

---

[*] Cross-cultural Leadership, International People Management Lecturer, Soft Skills Trainer, Researcher, Podcaster, Berlin, Germany.

analysis of English-language neologisms of the cultural-linguistic sphere of modern life (Shtaltovna, 2015). Quantitative analysis of the English derivation processes (2000-2015) in the cultural life sphere is reported in further publications (Shtaltovna, 2015b). Epistemology and parametric features of the «DEMOCRATIZATION» concept in English studies as well as the analysis of the definitional models and conceptual substrate of the «DEMOCRATIZATION» concept were published in 2018 (Shtaltovna, 2015c) as well as separating the use of the concept in the political and social discourses. As of 2016, the Use of the concept "Democratization" in Higher Education continued the research and its application in strategy writing and road mapping for Universities development (Shtaltovna, 2016).

Neology and sociolinguistics are at the crossroads of analysis for the democratization processes and need an integral approach combined with the concept studies to understand linguistic democratization dynamics fully. The research of the English neologisms being driven by sociolinguistic factors, especially after 2000 and the "Y2K Millenium bug", amplified number of the linguistic innovations and neologisms (Crystall, McFedries, Zatsnyi, Makhachashvili, Yenikeeva) as the signs of highly dynamic development of the English language system.

In this previously unpublished research, we will focus on sociolinguistics and pragmatics of the English-speaking youth dialect neologisms that can be illustrations for the four functional parameters of the language.

Functional parameters of contemporary English democratization

The study of the functional linguistic parameters one can find within the competence of pragmalinguistics. It distinguishes the following functions of language, according to Arnold (2002, p.8): **cognitive-communicative** function of language and **pragmatic** with all other sub-functions, namely:

- **emotive** function, i.e. with the transfer of feelings of the speaker,
- **voluntative** function, i.e. with the expression of will and motivation of the addressee to the desired action,
- **appellative** function, i.e. attracting the listener's attention, encouraging him to perceive the message,
- **vocative function,** in situations where utterances are not the transmission of messages but only a manifestation of attention to the presence of another person (for example, in the formulas of politeness),
- **aesthetic** function, i.e. with an impact on aesthetic sense.

The democratization of language includes the emancipation of language. It aims at changing hierarchical structures to establish a new, more democratic structure that aims at eradicating the dominance of one group over another to make legitimacy, equality, and the right to use language accessible to all. A sign of democratization is the expansion of the language field, which speakers perceive as acceptable for language use and which includes variability in contrast to the strict and well-defined rules of the standard language. Another sign of democratization of language is the use of variant and non-standard forms in various official sources and areas to raise the latter's status as valuable media resources for modern, democratic society (Huss and Lindgren 2011, p.2-3, 7-8).

The democratization of the literary language of the late XX-early XXI centuries is characterized by the active expansion of the functional linguo-sphere of English-speaking life - technological, social, socio-political, cultural, and scientific. The Internet provided personal access to the world's information heritage and introduced the possibility of having a private platform (s) for self-expression, self-identification, creation, and formation of personal information flows. The growth of practical individual needs in the nomination of new realities caused by the information-technical and technological development of the logosphere, as well as the openness of society, provoked changes in the development / of society; we observe the formation and functioning of sociolects.

The natural consequence of the shift from the canonized artistic language was the movement and mixing of linguistic and stylistic layers, intensification of the elements of colloquial style, dialectal variations, vernacular and dialectal language, reduced, vulgar, slang vocabulary, stylistic and genre syncretism, and interstitialism. It is evident that the new patterns of nominations, in turn, provide a continuous intensive creation of neological phrases and lexemes.

The peculiarities of neologisms' use are determined not only by the semantic competence of the speaker. It is not only responsible for the correlation of the sign and the word but also the pragmatic one, which provides a permanent connection between the speaker and the sign. Pragmatic parameters of neologisms most fully manifest in Internet discourse, characterized by constantly updating lexical vocabulary. This feature is since Internet discourse is inherently a heterogeneous phenomenon that integrates the characteristics of other types of discourse and covers all spheres of society. Therefore, functional analysis of discursive neologisms is an essential aspect of studying neologisms.

The linguistic concept of "neologism" covers a wide range of phenomena at the lexical-semantic level of language, and the problems of studying neology become especially important following new trends in the development of modern English. The emergence of new lexical units is a complex, multifaceted process that indicates the dynamics of language development. The variety of lexical and semantic neoplasms creates significant difficulties in determining the most characteristic features of neologisms, which would help to distinguish them from other innovations because the linguistic literature uses a variety of terms to denote lexical neoplasms: new vocabulary, lexical innovation, new word, neologism, neologism innovation, occasionalism, uncodified vocabulary, potential word, actual derivative, etc.

We will consider neologisms as new words, phrases, and meanings of words and phrases that have arisen in a certain period, are perceived as new units by the collective linguistic consciousness of native speakers and are gradually integrated into the language system. Neological pragmatic parameters most deeply manifest in media discourse, characterized by attempts to deepen and clarify information and give the semantic-pragmatic content greater efficiency and expressiveness, leading to the constant development of lexical vocabulary.

Lexical stylistics studies the components of the contextual meanings of words, especially their expressive, emotional, and evaluative potential and their relation to different functional and stylistic layers. Dialect words, terms, slang words, colloquial words and expressions, neologisms, archaisms, foreign words, expressive potential of some word-formation models, some types of abbreviations, and word-formation models (Arnold 2002, p.14) are studied in terms of their interaction with different conditions of the context, in our research in the context of democratization impact on the language system – reducing the stylistic distance between oral and spoken and written areas of its functioning; expanding the range of speakers and public use of literary language; expanding opportunities for linguistic self-expression of the individual; active search for new means of expression and expression in the conditions of competition between different media to win the readership and audience (Taranenko, p. 33). Democratization of language is described as an "opportunity for representatives of the people to create and put into circulation words and phrases that might be incorrectly spelled, may be dialectal, borrowed or highly specialized and not be socially condemned for their use in public, including in the media or Internet communication" (Shtaltovna, 2014).

Pragmatic parameters of neologisms are most fully manifested in Internet discourse, characterized by constantly updating lexical vocabulary. Linguists assign words to stylistically marked vocabulary, considering their dialectal nature, terminology, emotional colouring, and socially limited use. Stylistically marked words outnumber neutral vocabulary. That is, the sign of stylistic labelling of vocabulary is directly related to particular layers of vocabulary – dialectisms, professionalisms, terms, jargon, slang, and emotionally coloured words.

Yuri Zatsny notes that recently there has been a tendency towards "a certain democratization even of the British literary norm", and social dialects, which in English are often combined under the term "slang" are essential "internal sources of enrichment for the English language, and dictionaries still include slang to various categories of "standard" vocabulary and phraseology, especially neologisms (Zatsny, p.5). Zatsny also speaks of the current trend of "augmenting the stylistic status" for new language units: "In the 2003 edition of Collins' dictionary, more than 70 words that were considered taboo, vulgarisms in the previous edition (2000), were already marked as units of slang and colloquial vocabulary."

Among social dialects, the youth dialect (slang) stands out the most, a lexicon within the English language. The purpose of youth slang is to oppose oneself to the "system"; therefore, such features as colloquial and often familiar colouring, conformism, decentralization, personification, and individualization, as components of democratization, become signs of this linguistic phenomenon. Youth slang mainly aims at the following elements: a person, his clothes, appearance, leisure, housing, and other categories. This type of slang is "unstable" (i.e. changeable) compared to others due to the change in generations and the history and culture of each country.

The high level of dynamism and mobility of lexical and semantic composition in youth slang focuses on specific conceptual models of the low register, satirical, evaluative, pejorative type of high level of expressiveness. Nominative neologisms as the product of spontaneous, sometimes primitive word formation define new concepts for adolescents. Expressive neologisms denote already known phenomena and concepts. Language game involves manipulating the actual language to create a specific effect (comic, exposing, conceptual, protective).

Functional parameters of the democratization of the English language can be also categorized according to 4 **functions of identification, nomination, description, and differentiation,** as presented below (Figure 2), with examples of the innovative dialectisms in the youth dialect of contemporary English. This research illustrates these functions by youth dialectal neologisms extracted from the list of 5,452 English-language neologisms selected by continuous sampling from journalistic sources (The New York Times, The Guardian, The Times, The Washington Post, Chicago Tribune, etc.) and Internet resources (wordspy.com, very-clever.com, Readersheds.co.uk) for the period 1990-2015.

Identifying function as distinguishing 'us vs. them', seen as archetypal for adolescents who are discovering the world and enables a group of people with shared aims, beliefs, ideas, and interests to create a community, an English-speaking youth community in this case:

> **nico-teen** (n. A teenager who smokes cigarettes.)
> **alpha-girl** (n. The dominant member in a group of girls; a girl who bullies other girls.)
> **promzilla** (n. A high school girl who, while planning for her prom, becomes exceptionally selfish, difficult, and obnoxious.)
> **screenager** (n. A young person who has grown up with, and is therefore entirely comfortable with, a world of screens, particularly televisions, computers, ATMs, cell phones, and so on.)
> **Potterhead** (n. A person who is a big fan of the Harry Potter series of books.)
> **parachute kids** (n. Children sent to a new country to live alone or with a caregiver while their parents remain in their home country.).

The nominative function is expressed through the need to name new or specific phenomena in the life of teenagers. The name given allows youth to fix everything already cognizable and remain in consciousness:

> **Promposal** (n. An invitation to a prom, particularly one that is elaborate, unusual, or performed in a public place.)
> **Scratchiti** (n. A form of graffiti in marks are etched into windows and other glass surfaces.)
> **bullycide** (n. The suicide of a child that occurs after that child has been bullied or harassed.)
> **shoegaze** (v. To play an instrument, especially a guitar, with one's head down, as though gazing at one's shoes.)
> **social networking fatigue** (n. Mental exhaustion and stress caused by creating and maintaining an excessive number of accounts on social networking sites.)
> **hurried child syndrome** (n. A condition in which parents overschedule their children's lives, push them hard for academic success, and expect them to behave and react as miniature adults.)

The descriptive function is expressed by giving extra details defining and distinguishing a noun from a group of such and in the youth can be illustrated by the following dialectical innovations:

> **junk sleep** (n. Low-quality sleep caused by disruptions from nearby electronic devices such as cell phones, computers, and TVs.),
> **Pubilect** (n. A dialect unique to teenagers.);

antilanguage (n. A collection of words and phrases used to exclude outsiders from a particular group and to disguise the group's activities);

zitcom (n. A television sitcom aimed at or featuring teenagers),

Juvenoia (n. The baseless and exaggerated fear that the Internet and current social trends are having negative effects on children),

404 (adj. Out of touch or ignorant.),

lad lit (n. A literary genre that features books written by men and focusing on young, male characters, particularly those who are selfish, insensitive, and afraid of commitment),

grey-sky thinking (n. Negative or pessimistic thoughts, ideas, or solutions).

Differential function, the function of distinguishing other people who do not belong to a group like them, involves evaluation, and is therefore inseparable from the evaluative function:

Twilight mom (n. A mother who is a fan of the "Twilight" series of vampire novels.),

askable parent (n. A parent who is willing to answer their child's questions and who encourages their child to ask questions, particularly about sex.),

Millennial Generation (n. The generation born in 1978 or later),

Camgirl (n. A girl or young woman who broadcasts live pictures of herself over the web),

kidult (n. A middle-aged person who continues to participate in and enjoy youth culture),

Himbo (n. A man who is good-looking, but unintelligent or superficial),

digital native (n. A person who grew up in a world with computers, mobile phones, and other digital devices.),

wombat (adj. Profoundly uninteresting or useless - Waste Of Money, Brains And Time).

Having analyzed the chosen material, we conclude that all lexical-semantic and functional features and word-formation models of neologisms work in the slang layer, as explained by the high role of neologization with a high degree of expression as well as the tendency to individualization and originality, belonging to other age or social groups.

In summary, it should be noted that youth slang arises from the need for verbal self-identification, while increasing linguistic expression significantly expands the expression of the English language system, acting as a way of verbal communication, i.e. performing differential, descriptive, nominative, communicative and identifiable.

Discussion

Recently more research on linguistic democratization especially in the English language is being published and seen from different perspectives, as Hiltunen & Loureiro-Porto (2020) are reviewing previous synchronic and diachronic work studies on democratization in different varieties of English, especially vividly described in phenomenological neoanglistics (Makhachashvili, 2016). The corpus-based study considers differences between the more personal, more spoken-like, and more colloquial blogs component (Kranich, Hampel, & Bruns, 2020) and the study of the evidence of conversationalization and democratization within the changing contextual environment of the radio shows. A DemLang project focuses on diachronic research of the Democratization, Mediatization and Language Practices in Britain, 1700–1950 (Palander-Collin et al., 2020) and proceeds to sociohistorical contextualization of British English is seen as a sign of the democratization (Palander-Collin & Nevala, 2020). Democratization of the Italian linguistic loans is studied as a demonstration of democratization of the Italian language (Moskalenko, 2017) and Processes of Language Democratization in Contemporary Ukraine examines Presidential Speeches (Nedashkivska, 2006). Even though the Natural Language interfaces are now studied to be democratized, the research goes towards Democratizing Data Science with Natural Language Interfaces (Su, 2018). Looking forward to the Metaverse and Internet 5.0 democratization, once we bridge the digital divide and bring open access to scientific achievements to be able to make a meta-analysis including all the linguistic democratization studies of the Modern Languages.

Conclusions

Democratization and liberalization as common causes and engines of the linguistic and literary processes shape the fashion for new words and phrases and intensify the personal search for new tools for the formation of expression. Democratization of the language standard, essentially the goal of restandardization, includes the idea of democratization of language norms.

New patterns of nominations, in turn, provide a continuous intensive creation of neological phrases and tokens, which grow into texts and intertexts, creating a new linguistic discourse, which in turn intensifies the search for new means of expression, which is a partial manifestation of the general laws of the modern linguistic system, in particular tendencies to democratization, intellectualization, the actualization of nominations.

The democratization of language can be reflected in the extension of standards and the inclusion of oral and written invariants and neologisms at different levels of language use, as well as in official sources. The limits of what is (or is not) acceptable, or part of a standard, are greatly expanded to include dialectal, sociolectal, borrowed, newly created elements, or elements of narrow, particular use.

Every native speaker in a democratic society has the right to an equal contribution to the development of language at both formal and informal levels, so the involvement of a broader base of linguistic variations ensures sustainable and successful development and expansion of standard language and includes bilateral vertical cooperation of all national representatives, regional and local language community. Democratization of language is the process of reaching the broader opportunity to create and put lexical items that are not orthographically correct, can be dialectal, borrowed, or highly specialized, and not be condemned or stigmatized for their use, including in the media or Internet communication.

English-language innovations of the 21st century are the means of expression of democratization processes through such trends as the tendency to complicate, enrich the language structure, condensation, abbreviation, the tendency to use stylistically different language forms with different emotional and expressive meanings. Having analyzed the stylistic marking and functional parameters of the postmodern period's English abbreviations, acronyms, terminological innovations, dialectisms, pejorative neologisms, and euphemisms of neologic vocabulary, we subset the youth slang and its functional parameters. We can note that youth slang arises from the need for verbal self-identification and expression as a way of verbal communication, i.e. performing differential, descriptive, nominative, and identifying functions.

References

1.   Arnold, Y. V. (2010). Stylystyka. Sovremennyi anhlyiskyi yazyk. [Contemporary English].

2.   Crystal, D. (2001). A linguistic revolution. Education, Communication and Information, 1(2), 93-7.

3.   Crystal, D. (2005). The scope of Internet linguistics. In Proceedings of American Association for the Advancement of Science Conference; American Association for the Advancement of Science Conference, Washington, DC, USA (pp. 17-21).

4.   Kranich, S., Hampel, E., & Bruns, H. (2020). Changes in the modal domain in different varieties of English as potential effects of democratization. Language Sciences, 79, 101271. https://doi.org/10.1016/j.langsci.2020.101271

5.   Herrero, L. (2011). *Homo Imitans: The Art of Social Infection: Viral Change in Action.* Meetingminds Publishing.

6.   Hiltunen, T., & Loureiro-Porto, L. (2020). Democratization of Englishes: Synchronic and diachronic approaches. Language Sciences, 79, 101275. https://doi.org/10.1016/j.langsci.2020.101275

7.   Huss, L. and A.-R. Lindgren. 2011. Introduction: Defining language emancipation. *International Journal of the Sociology of Language* 209: 1-15. https://doi.org/10.1515/ijsl.2011.018

8.   Makhachashvili, R. K. (2003). "Kompiuterni" novotvory suchasnoi anhliiskoi movy: do problemy sotsiolinhvistychnoi typolohizatsii. ["Computer" innovations of the modern English language: to the problem of sociolinguistic typology].

9.   Makhachashvili, R. (2010). *Linguophilosophic Parameters of English Innovations in Technosphere.* Cambridge Scholars Publishing.

10.   Makhachashvili, R. K. (2016). Fenomenolohichna neoanhlistyka: teoretyko-metodolohichni zasady. [Phenomenological neo-English studies: theoretical and methodological foundations] BBK 81.2 Anhl-43 A 64, 104.

11.   McFedries, P. (2022). Word Spy - The Word Lover's Guide to New Wordsby Logophilia Limited. https://wordspy.com/index.php?tag=all-by-category

12. Moskalenko, A. O. (2017). Italian loans in the course of time as the demonstration of democratization of the Italian language. Molodyy vchenyy, (5), 174-180.

13. Nedashkivska, A. (2006). Presidential Speech and Processes of Language Democratization in Contemporary Ukraine. Australian Slavonic and East European Studies, 20(1-2), 39-65.

14. Palander-Collin, M., Nevala, M., Pahta, P., Nurmi, A., & Tyrkkö, J. (2020). Democratization and language practices: Introducing the DEMLANG project. https://doi.org/10.1075/pbns.195

15. Palander-Collin, M., & Nevala, M. (2020). Person reference and democratization in British English. Language Sciences, 79, 101265. https://doi.org/10.1016/j.langsci.2019.101265

16. Shtaltovna, Yu. A. (2014). Vplyv demokratyzatsii na leksyko-semantychni protsesy v kulturnii sferi zhyttia suchasnoi anhliiskoi movy. [The impact of democratization on lexical-semantic processes in the cultural sphere of life of the modern English language]. Nova filolohiia, (64), 208-213.

17. Shtaltovna Yu. (2015). Influence of democratization on derivative processes in the cultural sphere of modern English language. In «The Fifth European Conference on Languages, Literature and Linguistics». Proceedings of the Conference. (pp. 29-34). «East-West» Association for Advanced Studies and Higher Education GmbH. Vienna.

18. Shtaltovna, Yu. (2015). Linguistic and cognitive, semantic, structural and functional parameters of the English language democratization (based on the late 20th-early 21st century English innovations), (Doctoral dissertation), ZNU.

19. Shtaltovna, Yu. (2015). Epistemolohiia ta parametrychni vlastyvosti kontseptu DEMOCRATIZATION v anhlomovnykh studiiakh [Epistemology and parametric properties of the DEMOCRATIZATION concept in English-language studies]. Aktualni pytannia humanitarnykh nauk, (11), 147-154.

20. Shtaltovna, Yu. A. (2015). Paradyhma strukturno-semantychnykh poliv kontseptu democratization v suchasnii anhliiskii movi [The paradigm of structural and semantic fields of the concept of democratization in modern English.]. Naukovi zapysky Natsionalnoho universytetu Ostrozka akademiia. Seriia: Filolohichna, (55), 291-293. https://doi.org/10.25264/15.04.2020

21. Shtaltovna, Y. A. (2016). Education environment democratization as a higher education development strategy. Electronic Scientific Professional Journal "Open Educational E-Environment of Modern University", (2), 273-282. https://doi.org/10.28925/2414-0325.2016.2.d27382

22.   Shtaltovna, Yu. (2018). The pursuit of democratization in education-knowing where to go. Concept analysis for the correct use of the term democratization of education. Open Educational E-Environment of Modern University, (4), 74-82. https://doi.org/ 10.28925/2414-0325.2018.4.7482

23.   Su, Y. (2018). Towards Democratizing Data Science with Natural Language Interfaces (Doctoral dissertation, UC Santa Barbara).

24.   Taranenko O.O. Kolokvializatsiia, substandartyzatsiia ta vulharyzatsiia yak kharakterni yavyshcha stylistyky suchasnoi ukrainskoi movy (z kintsia 1980-kh) [Colloquialization, substandardization, and vulgarization as characteristic phenomena of the stylistics of the modern Ukrainian language (since the late 1980s)] // Movoznavstvo. – 2002. – No 4-5, prodovzhennia – No 1, 2003.

25.   Yenikieieva, S. M. (2006). Systemnist i rozvytok slovotvoru suchasnoi anhliiskoi movy: monohrafiia. [Systematicity and development of the word-form of the modern English language: a monograph.] Zaporizhzhia: Zaporizkyi natsionalnyi universytet.

26.   Zatsnyi, Yu. A. (1998). Rozvytok slovnykovoho skladu suchasnoi anhliiskoi movy [Development of the vocabulary of the modern English language]. Zaporizhzhia: Zaporizkyi derzhavnyi universytet.

Author's bio

Dr. **Yuliya Shtaltovna** has presently been working as an Associate Lecturer at ISM International School of Management GmbH, Berlin, Germany. She has studied the Democratization of the Modern Ukrainian Language since 2006 and wrote a Master's thesis on the Ukrainian Language. At present, too, she is engaged with her study of the Democratization of the English Language within the Zaporizka School of Neology (ZNU) under the supervision of Prof. Rusudan Makhachashvili. Her focus of study is the concept of Studies and the Linguistic Parameters of the Democratization of the Contemporary English (2015).
    Dr. Yuliya Shtaltovna studied the Democratization of the Modern Ukrainian Language since 2006 and wrote a Master's thesis on the Ukrainian Language Democratization as presented in Contemporary Ukrainian Literature (2000-2007). In her Doctoral research, she continued her study of the Democratization of the English Language within the Zaporizka School of Neology (ZNU) under the supervision of Prof. Rusudan Makhachashvili by focusing on the concept studies and the linguistic parameters of the democratization of the Contemporary English (2015). As part of implementing the Democratization concept findings, she continued researching the Democratization concept for the Higher education strategic documents and road mapping at BGKU, Kyiv, Ukraine. Since 2017, she focuses on Soft Skills Development and Business Education Internationalization and Democratization in a number of Business Schools in Berlin. The spectrum of the subjects taught now is from Contemporary Leadership Culture and Social Skills to Intercultural Management and Transformation in the Global Environment. She is also an editorial advisor for the Gile

Journal of Skills Development (GJSD) and its annual international conference on Skills Development for Youth Employability (GILE4Youth).

Her thrust areas of research comprise Soft Skills Development and Business Education Internationalization and Democratization, Democratization of English and European languages, Intercultural Communication and Sociolinguistics, Discourse Studies and Concept Studies, Neology and Stylistics, Soft Skills Development and Assessment, Employability.

Dr. Yuliya Shtaltovna has 30+ research articles, several monograph chapters to her credit in at national as well as international level. She also got published two books: Enhancing students' digital competencies within the Employability module of the University of Europe's skills-based curricula (2021), Can a Skill be Measured or Assessed? 6-Level Skills Development Approach to Skill Assessment (2021).

N. Lazebna / D. Kumar (Ed.), Studies in Modern English, Würzburg, 2022, p. 117-124. DOI: 10.25972/WUP-978-3-95826-199-0-117

A Case Study of the Basic Learners' Struggles in Guessing from Context to Retain Words Learned

Zuraina Ali[*]

Abstract

Guessing meaning from context is a challenging strategy for Second Language Learners (SLLs). In using the strategy, research found that poor students or low proficiency learners struggled in their attempts to use it. Mainly, it was reported that it was due to their vocabulary knowledge was limited. In another aspect, retaining vocabulary learnt is also important. Such is essential since learning vocabulary does not mean knowing the definition only. Yet, learners must also be able to use the vocabulary as they engage in language skills such as reading, writing, speaking and listening. The study aims at finding the hindrances faced among poor students' using contextual clues in retaining vocabulary. The study employed a case study to collect data from two basic students studying at a tertiary level. The study found that their hindrances in guessing meaning contexts were due to their being confused in guessing meaning when reading a sentence. Also, it was found that they were not able to find clues since they lacked vocabulary to guess correctly. The study implied that guessing meaning from context required sizeable vocabulary knowledge. Therefore, more training is necessary to assist basic learners in being successful in guessing from contexts.

Keywords: contextual clues, basic learners, vocabulary, vocabulary retention, vocabulary knowledge

Introduction

Vaezi and Fallah (2010) define Contextual Clues as words that signal the meaning of a word in the text surrounding it. The clues help a learner arrive at a word's general meaning. Haastrup (1991, as cited in Hamada 2009), further, explains that Contextual Clues provide informed guesses as to the meaning of a word in the light of all available linguistic clues in combination with a learner's general knowledge of the world and awareness of context.

On a different note, most vocabulary is acquired by deriving word meaning from context (Beck & McKeown, 1991), a method that requires learners to compensate for limited knowledge (Oxford & Burry-Stock, 1995). Waring (2000) indicates that guessing the meaning of the unknown words from context is the most important vocabulary learning strategy for students at the tertiary level. Since teachers do not have enough time to teach every word,

---

[*] Associate Professor, Department of English, Centre for Modern Languages, University Malaysia Pahang, Pekan, Pahang, Malaysia.

those students do not understand in class, deducing meaning from context leaves students to guess the unknown words successfully. Unfortunately, he claims, teachers merely expect students to know how to guess well, yet thousands of students need help to be more successful at guessing (Waring, 2000).

Moreover, learning from context affects incidental vocabulary differently (Gu, 2003). Beginning L2 learners may have more trouble learning incidental vocabulary because of their inability to make sense of new words and their contexts (Gu, 2003). Yet, Robb (1989) argues that extensive reading may improve their effort in guessing from context since the activity is interesting. Also, teachers can instruct them to be aware of the linguistic information, for instance, parts of speech that are presented within a text – in order for them to be successful at guessing (Cheung, 2007). Thus, realising this, the aim of learning from context - creating the conditions for learners to learn independently of the teacher - can be achieved (Waring, 2000).

Previous studies reported guessing meaning from context was not preferred by students learning English (L2). Tat (2022) found that guessing meaning from context even though the lack of grammar knowledge made them not confident when reading. Coupled with their inability to master verb patterns and prepositions, guessing meaning from context was difficult for learners taking the Test of English for International Communication (TOEIC) – a standardized English test designed for professionals and students in learning the language.

There is a difference between good and poor learners in guessing. Thuỷ (2021) reported that learners with low English proficiency looked up unfamiliar words when guessing meaning from context. Instead, their counterparts made educated guesses when they identified words they were unknown. Also, the strategy 'Obtaining and Using Resources' was the only strategy concerning guessing meaning context used by the poor proficiency learners. Moreover, due to inadequate vocabulary knowledge, they relied on global strategies to make up their skills in guessing meaning from context. Interestingly, Huang (2021) reported that guessing meaning from contexts is a shortcut for high school students employed in his study. Yet, the researcher did not mention whether the use of shortcuts was among the poor or good learners.

The objective of the study

The study was conducted to identify the hindrances that poor English learners experienced when they were instructed to guess the meaning from context. Mainly, the hindrances relate to understanding their struggles when using the method to retain the vocabulary learned after they were exposed to a series of classes using the strategy. Therefore, a single research question was formulated in the current study. The research question is "What are the hindrances faced among basic learners of English guessing meaning from contexts in retaining vocabulary?".

Methodology

Research Design

The study employed a qualitative research design, specifically a case study, to collect the data in the current study. Cherry (2021) states that a case study is research conducted to identify an in-depth exploration of one person, group, or event. It attempts to find patterns and causes of behaviour among respondents. However, it needed to be cautious that findings from the study could not be generalised to a larger population since it was highly subjective (Cherry, 2021, para. 1).

Research Samples

The research samples were two basic learners studying engineering at a local university on the East Coast of Malaysia. In the current study, they were called basic learners because they obtained low scores in the tests carried out during their English class in that particular semester. The study employs purposive sampling. Samples are selected based on the judgement that they are typical or representative of the population (Fraenkel et al., 2011). They are believed to represent the first-year students, and therefore, able to provide the data that is needed for the study. In reporting, these students were identified using their pseudonyms – Dina and Fiza.

Research Instruments

Semi-structured interviews are employed to gauge students' opinions after completing the lessons, tests and questionnaires. The purpose of interviewing them is to elicit specific answers on their part after they received the vocabulary learning techniques (J. R. Fraenkel et al., 2012). Later, their responses will be compared and contrasted. Regarding validating the research instrument, a lecturer from CMLHS was consulted to validate the interview protocol for the basic learners. This was necessary since any instrument that is translated into another language must again be subjected to further analysis for validation (Birt et al., 2016). The only amendment proposed was requiring the interviewees to provide examples to illustrate their explanations. In terms of reliability for qualitative data, triangulation strengthens its reliability after quantitative data is collected and analysed (Merriam, 1998). However, the reporting of the quantitative parts was not presented in this writing.

Procedures for data collection and analysis

A few procedures took place in collecting and analysing the data in the current study. In undergoing the former, the researcher appointed a lecturer to teach as well as to guess meaning from contexts to the students. The teaching was conducted over a month during English class lessons. Besides that, three recall tests were conducted on the students. These tests were pre and post-tests and immediate recall tests. Before the interview, they were given a break of no lessons and tests to ensure they were afresh before the interview was conducted. During the interview session, the researcher called the two basic learners to interview them during class hours. In the data analysis, thematic coding was employed in that themes were formulated to represent the students' experiences of guessing meaning from contexts.

Analysis of the research

Two themes – 'Confusions Lead to Deviant Clues' 'Lacking the Richness of Words in Context to Provide Clues' – were identified concerning the hindrances of using Contextual Clues in retaining words learnt.

Confusions Lead to Deviant Clues

The two basic learners were required to answer questions in the test during the interview to identify how they guessed. It was found that they made wrong hunches about clues they chose when attempting to answer one of the test questions. In Dina's case, for example, she assumed that her guesses were correct because of the clues she claimed in the sentence, while in reality, it turned out to be a wrong judgement. The answer to item seven of Section B in Immediate Recall Test 2 – illustrated in the episode below – corresponded to her experience concerning this issue.

Dina:	Passing through the arch you enter an open courtyard - Area, I think is the answer ('Passing through the arch you enter an open courtyard' - *Area, sayafikirjawapannya*)
Teacher:	Why do you think that is the answer? (*Sebabapakamu rasa itulahjawapannya?*)
Dina:	"'Area' is a space. So, he passed the 'area' and go to the 'courtyard'. I think 'courtyard' is the clue". (*'Area' [ialah] kawasan. Jadi diamelepasikawasan itu dan pergike 'courtyard'. 'Courtyard' itu saya rasa clue dia*)
Teacher:	So, is that why your answer is area? (*Jadi, sebab itu jawapankamu 'area'?*)
Dina:	I just guess [giggles]. Then I see that the word is suitable for the sentence (*Saya cumatekasahaja [ketawa]. Lepas [i]tusayatengokperkataan [i]tusesuaidenganayat*).

Fiza, too made the wrong attempt in answering item five of Section B in Immediate Recall Test 2. She perceived that 'corn' and 'wheat' were the clues to the question and decided to choose 'watches' as the answer. However, she failed to realise that the word deviated from her guesses. The following is the transcription of the interview with Fiza:

Teacher:	Can you attempt Question Five? The hungry _____ are eating corn and wheat. So, what is the answer for the blank space? *(Bolehtakawakcuba buat soalannombor lima ni.* The hungry _____ are eating corn and wheat. *So apakahjawapan yang sesuai di tempatkosong?)*
Fiza:	[long pause] 'watches'
Teacher:	Watches? Okay. Can you tell me what is the word that give clue to you that makes you choose the answer; watches? *(Ok. Bolehtakkamuberitahusayaapakahperkataan yang memberi clue kepadakamu yang menyebabkankamupilihjawapanini*[watches]*).*
Fiza:	'Corn' and 'wheat'
Teacher:	So, how do you guess that 'watches' is the answer? (So, *macam mana kamu bole tekaitulah (watches) jawapannya?)*
Fiza:	[long pause]…the word 'penonton' means 'watches'… so, 'watches' eat 'corn' and 'wheat' [giggles] *(penontonialah watches… so, penontonmakan 'corn' and 'wheat').*

Lacking the Richness of Words in Context to Provide Clues

The basic learners claimed that not all words that appear in the context were rich enough to provide them with clues needed to determine the meaning of the target words. The lack of sufficient information for guessing impeded them in identifying the correct meaning of the target words. Since they could not figure out the meaning of the target word, they could not retain it. Fiza explained:

> Mmm... I think every sentence has the clue. But if we [in the first place] didn't understand the sentence…then we might not know the meaning of the target words.

Dina added that she claimed that it was a problem for her when she was asked to guess the meaning of words, due to her inability to understand the meaning of the sentence. As a result, she could not work out the clues for the sentence, although she realised that they might help her guessing the meaning of the target words. She cited her experience:

> The problem [in using Contextual Clues] is when we didn't understand the sentence. [We] didn't know the clues itselves although we know that they might help us in guessing meaning of the word.

Discussions

Basic learners found that guessing was difficult since they claimed that words in a particular sentence were insufficient to help them identify the meaning of the target words. Laufer (1990) suggests that the learners must know 95% of the words to make them understand the text. In fact, there should be no more than one unknown word in about every 20 words read (Schmitt, 2000).

Taking these points into consideration, in the present study, contextual clues were provided in synonyms, explanations and definitions, among others, during the exercises. These types of sentences could help them in guessing and, in the end, could assist them in retaining the meaning of the words. This finding disagrees with Carnine et al., (1984) claim that students were more capable of figuring out the meaning of unfamiliar words when the similar meaning of the target words were provided. However, caution must be taken in interpreting the finding because this was the experience of the basic learners, and therefore it could not be generalised.

Conclusion

In conclusion, two themes emerged from the analysis of data. There were 'Confusions Lead to Deviant Clues' and 'Lacking the Richness of Words in Context to Provide Clues'. The study implied that more training on guessing from context is needed to help the basic learners overcome their difficulties. However, the root of the matter is the most essential step in improving the use of the strategy among them. It is suggested that there need to be some principles in learning vocabulary. Students need to follow the procedures that the teacher instructs. Only then can they accommodate their strategy when guessing meaning from context. Nevertheless, this finding enhances our understanding that matching learners' level of competencies is important to promote successful vocabulary learning, especially in guessing from contexts. This requires teachers to identify appropriate classroom activities with students' abilities upon using the strategy in learning and consequently retaining words learned.

References

1.   Birt, L., Scott, S., Cavers, D., Campbell, C., & Walter, F. (2016). Member Checking: A Tool to Enhance Trustworthiness or Merely a Nod to Validation? Qualitative Health Research, 26. https://doi.org/10.1177/1049732316654870

2.   Carnine, D., Kameenui, E. J., & Coyle, G. (1984). Utilisation of contextual information in determining the meaning of unfamiliar words. Reading Research Quarterly, 188–204.

3.   Cherry, K. (2021). What is a Case Study? https://www.verywellmind.com/how-to-write-a-psychology-case-study-2795722

4.   Fraenkel, J. R., Wallen, N. E., & Hyun, H. H. (2012). How to design and evaluate research in education. McGraw-hill New York.

5.   Fraenkel, J., Wallen, N., & Hyun, H. (2011). How to Design and Evaluate Research in Education. In Journal of American Optometric Association (Vol. 60).

6.   Gu, Y., P. (2003). Vocabulary Learning in A Second Language: Person, Task, Context and Strategies. TESL- EJ, 7 (2), 1- 25.

7.   Huang, C. (2021). A Study On The Vocabulary Learning Stragies Of High School Students In Jiangsu Province. International Journal of Social Science and Economic Research, 6(4), 1133–1142.

8.   Robb, T. (1989). Extensive Reading vs. Skills Building in an EFL Context, Reading in A Foreign Language, 5 (2), 239-251.

9.   Laufer, B. (1990). Easy and Difficulty in Vocabulary Learning: Some Teaching Implications,Foreign Language Annals, 23, 147-156.

10.   Merriam, S., B. (1998). Qualitative Research and Case Study Applications in Education, California: Josey-Bass Inc.

11.   Oxford, R. L., & Burry-Stock, J. A. (1995). Assessing the use of language learning strategies worldwide with the ESL/EFL version of the Strategy Inventory for Language Learning (SILL). System, 23(1), 1–23.

12.   Tat, H. N. (2022). TOEIC Reading Test: EFL Non-Majors' Attitudes Towards and Perceptions of Reading Comprehension and Reading Test-Taking Strategies. Eastern Journal of Languages, Linguistics and Literatures, 3(1), 1–23.

13.   Thuỷ, N. (2021). Reading Strategies Used By Students Of Different Levels Of English Reading Proficiency. VNU Journal of Foreign Studies, 37(4).

14.   Waring, R. (2000). How to Get Your Students to Use their Dictionaries Effectively from http://www1.harenet.ne.jp/~waring/vocab/dictionary/dictionary.htm.

15.   Oxford, R. L., & Burry-Stock, J. A. (1995). Assessing the use of language learning strategies worldwide with the ESL/EFL version of the Strategy Inventory for Language Learning (SILL). System, 23(1), 1–23.

16.   Schmitt, N. (2000). Vocabulary in Language Teaching, NY: Cambridge University Press.

17.   Vaezi, S. & Fallah, N. (2010) Rigorous and Multifaceted Vocabulary Instructional Program, European Journal of Social Sciences, 14 (2).

Author's bio

Dr. Zuraina Ali has presently been working as an Associate Professor of English at University of Malaysia, Pahang. She is the co-author of many English textbooks that have been prescribed at university level. She has also a number of research papers to her credit in National as well as International journals. Her thrust areas of research comprise vocabulary learning and technology used in the Second Language Acquisition (SLA). Besides, she is also a trainer of English courses for adult and research methodology. She has also conducted language and research courses training.

Editors

Nataliia Lazebna, Privat Dozent, Dr. Habil. TEFL Metodology Department, New Philological Institute, Julius-Maximilians University of Wuerzburg, Germany, was born on May 15, 1985 in Zaporizhzhia, Ukraine. She defended her Habilitation Project at Zaporizhzhia National University, Zaporizhzhia, Ukraine, in 2021, in the Field of Germanic languages. She obtained degree of Habilitated Doctor of Philological Sciences in the field of Germanic Languages (Confirmed by Zentralstelle für ausländisches Bildungswesen, Bonn, 21/04/2022, with the following Berufliche Anerkennung: habilitierter Wissenschaftler). She obtained her Ph.D. in Philological Sciences in the field of Germanic Languages in 2013 at Donetsk National University, Ukraine. Participated in AE E-Teacher Programs. TESOL Methodology certified (March, 2019). Alumni Cascade OPEN Courses with Colleagues (August - November, 2020). AE E-Teacher TESOL Methodology MOOC Facilitator at University of Maryland Baltimore County (February, 2020). For 15 years she has been working as Associate Professor at Department of Theory and Practice of Translation, Zaporizhzhia National Polytechnic University. The author of more than 50 academic journal articles, conference proceedings, and students' guidelines. The Official Opponent at 8 thesis defenses. The reviewer of vocabularies, monographs, and other printed scientific materials. An experienced translator and academic writer in the American and UK Companies.

Dinesh Kumar has presently been working as an Assistant Professor of English at Dyal Singh College, Karnal (INDIA) for the last 15 years. Besides, 40 research papers to his credit in reputed National as well as International Journals, his thrust areas of research comprise of Feminism, Dalit Literature, Comparative Literature, Commonwealth Literature, postcolonialism, Linguistic, Eco-feminism, Translation Study and Postmodernism. In addition to it, he has also contributed 20 book chapters on different topics. He has three books to his credit as a sole author- George Orwell's Social Vision: A Critical Study (ISBN 978-93-87646-79-7); and Voices in Literature. (ISBN 978-93-87276-79-6), Feministic Ethos in Pre-Independence and Post- Independence Indian Literature: A Comprehensive Study from Lambert Publication, Germany (ISBN 978-620-3-921908). He has also reviewed two books of foreign professors-first, English Language as Mediator of Human-Machine Communication by Natalia Lazebna, Associate Professor, Zaporizhizhia Polytechnic University, Ukraine with ISBN 978-81-948672-1-0. and the second is a poetry book, Drops of Intensity by an Italian poet, Gerlinde Staffler. Being an active member in the editorial boards of different National and International journals since 2014, he is rendering his services as an editor and a reviewer in national and International Journals.